Library of
Davidson College

# THE ROMANS

ON THE

# RIVIERA AND THE RHONE

# THE ROMANS

ON THE

# RIVIERA AND THE RHONE

A SKETCH OF THE CONQUEST OF LIGURIA
AND THE ROMAN PROVINCE

BY

W. H. (BULLOCK) HALL, F.R.G.S.

CORRESPONDING MEMBER OF THE LITERARY AND SCIENTIFIC SOCIETIES OF
NICE AND DRAGUIGNAN, AND OF THE SOCIETÉ ÉDUENNE OF AUTUN.

ARES PUBLISHERS INC.
CHICAGO          MCMLXXIV

937.1
H181w

Unchanged Reprint of the Edition:
London, 1898.
ARES PUBLISHERS INC.
150 E. Huron Street
Chicago, Illinois 60611
Printed in the United States of America
International Standard Book Number:
0-89005-02208
Library of Congress Catalog Card Number:
74-77871

TO MY FRIEND

PROFESSOR RIDGEWAY
OF THE UNIVERSITY OF CAMBRIDGE

IN GRATEFUL RECOGNITION OF
ASSISTANCE AND ENCOURAGEMENT
AFFORDED THROUGHOUT THE COMPOSITION
OF THIS WORK

# PREFACE.

HAVING enjoyed for the last twelve years the privilege of wintering on the north-western shores of the Mediterranean, I have turned them to account by following up in every direction the tracks left by the Romans on the French and Italian Rivieras. Nor have my explorations been confined to the coast, but have been extended north of the Apennines as far as the Po in Italy, and in France have included the seldom-visited valleys of the Durance and the Drôme. It is in the hope of throwing some light of local colouring on to an obscure field of Roman history, that I am tempted to offer this sketch to the public. For mainly owing to the irreparable loss of the books of Livy's history treating of the conquest of Provence (the Roman Provincia), we are left very much in the dark on that important episode in Roman history. Nothing but the intimate acquaintance with the locality which the writer possesses has rendered it possible to eke out the slender materials available, for the construction of any kind of bridge over the gap in Roman history between the narratives of Livy and Caesar; and some bridge is indispensable, to connect the broken ends of the two narratives. For Caesar's Gallic War, with which the student usually begins his acquaintance with Gaul, is really only the second act of the drama of the Roman conquest of that country. It is indispensable, for instance, to be forewarned that (1) the '*Omnis* Gallia' of

Caesar means Gallia with the Rhone Valley left out, as already conquered and reduced to a Province; (2) that the inroad of the Helvetii into Gaul, so ruthlessly arrested and repulsed by Caesar, was looked upon as threatening a repetition of the Cimbro-Teuton invasion, which had so nearly overwhelmed Italy less than half a century earlier; (3) that the driving of Ariovistus back across the Rhine showed that Caesar's eagle-eye saw at a glance where the real danger lay, and that it was better policy to encounter Germany in Alsace than on the Rhone or in Provence.

Passing my winters as I do within sight of the ruins of Forum Julii, which is really a Rome in miniature, I have been imbibing an atmosphere as completely Roman, as if I had been living on the outskirts of the Eternal City.

In fact I have often had to ask myself, can it be that the long line of mellow arches, which I see there striding across the plain, are other than those of the Claudian Aqueduct, and that those brown-hooded shepherds, sheltering with their flocks from the fierce rays of the midday sun under spreading stone-pines, are anything else than the familiar figures and features of the Roman Campagna?

When, escorted by the arches of the aqueduct—those *avant-coureurs* of the ruined city,—you approach the entrance, where the Porta Romana once stood, and gaze on the picturesque outline of the walls still standing, though in ruin, and the Roman towers, cutting clear against the western sky, you have before you a scene of concentrated Roman ingredients, unsurpassable even at Rome.

One has often to ask oneself, why is it, that when once the Romans have set their seal on a place, it is redeemed for ever from dullness, and that its desolation becomes more eloquent than words can express?

Somewhat to the author's own surprise, his work, which originated in musings over the ruins of Forum

Julii, has taken the form of a sketch of the expansion of Italy into Gaul through the Roman conquest of Liguria, which prepared the way for Caesar's Gallic Wars.

It was only by degrees that the author became aware how much wider was the ancient Liguria than the strip of Italian coast to which it is limited by modern geographers. He soon discovered that at Frejus he was in a centre, which was Ligurian before it became Roman, and that he was located at the most convenient point on the coast for exploring the whole of ancient Liguria, which extended from the Rhone on the west across the Alps as far east as the line of the Trebia, prolonged across the Apennines by the valley of the Magra to the Mediterranean.

In Gaul, it reached from the coast inland as far as the level of the Isère, and in Italy up to that of the upper half of the course of the Po, and even beyond it[1].

The references in the text and notes will make it clear that the author has had occasion to draw more on foreign than on British sources for assistance in the composition of this sketch. While French, Germans and Italians have dealt with the different branches of his subject, the author is unacquainted with any English work dealing specially with it.

Although reluctantly compelled to point out the serious errors into which M. Lentheric has fallen on the subject of the Via Aurelia, the author is glad to acknowledge the pleasure he has derived from the rest of his work which is known to the French as *La Provence Maritime*, and to the British reader as *The Riviera Ancient and Modern*.

For a detailed account of Forum Julii the author refers his readers to the "Histoire de Frejus" by J. A. Aubenas, to which the author is himself much indebted.

In Herzog's Historia Provinciae Narbonensis (1863)

[1] In the days of Justinian, Milan was considered the capital of Liguria. See Gibbon, Milman's Edition, Vol. IV. p. 57.

the student who wishes to go deeper in the subject will find an admirable and scholarly work.

The author offers his best thanks to Mr Jenkinson, Cambridge University Librarian, for unfailing courtesy in supplying him with works of reference, as also to Mr A. S. Murray and to Mr W. R. Wilson of the British Museum. He has also to express his obligation to Mr E. S. Shuckburgh for the use of his translation of Polybius and other assistance, and to Professor Rhys of Oxford for valuable hints. He is indebted to Mr A. Rogers of the Cambridge University Library for the compilation of the Index at the end of the volume.

The author has finally to tender his best thanks to Mr H. J. Edwards of Trinity College, for reading over the proofs while the work was passing through the Press.

# LIST OF MAPS AND PLANS.

The Riviera, Provence (Roman Province) and regions adjacent.

The mouths of the Rhone.

Plan of Marseilles. Ancient and Modern.

Plan of Frejus (Forum Julii). Ancient and Modern.

Section of the Table of Peutinger.

# THE ROMANS ON THE RIVIERA AND THE RHONE.

## CHAPTER I.

### INTRODUCTORY.

BEFORE bringing the Roman actors on to the stage, it will be well to take a preliminary glance at the early distribution of races in Liguria and Gaul. For, as far as I know, there are very few persons on this side the Channel, who are at all aware of the extremely subversive views on the subject, which are rapidly gaining ground in France. Had I been writing only thirty years ago, it would hardly have been necessary even to refer to the presence of traces of pre-historic man in the regions under review. But the recent discoveries in the field of pre-historic archaeology have been too important to be left entirely unmentioned, even in a work professing to deal exclusively with history. The future indeed seems to belong to the physical investigators, who brush aside in a somewhat high-handed manner the old fashioned history, which is based mainly on texts.

Largely in consequence of physical evidence the ideas on the subject of the earliest inhabitants of Gaul, which were embodied in the works of the late Amédée Thierry, and which prevailed in France so recently as the date of the publication of the *Life of Julius Caesar* by Napoleon III., are undergoing a radical change.

## INTRODUCTORY.

For there is no trace in those works of any perception of the theory that the Gauls never really formed the groundwork of the population in the country we call France[1]. It is now beginning to dawn upon the French mind, that as an invading minority of German Franks have given their name to modern France, so its ancient name Gallia was derived from invading Galli—a race resembling Germans in type—who subdued, without displacing, the indigenous population.

It seems evident that, if the majority of the inhabitants of France were of Gallic origin, they ought to be tall and fair. Whereas—and that more especially in the generally believed-to-be purely Celtic regions of the west of France, they are as a matter of fact found to be small and dark. The skulls too and skeletons derived from the tombs in western France are mostly round and short, instead of being long and tall.

So whatever race-feud exists between French and Germans is not to be attributed to the Celtic element in the French people. For, in spite of their difference in language Celts and Germans are of kindred blood. Strabo, p. 196[2].

The first modern writer to draw public attention to the above anomaly was the Baron Roger de Belloguet, whose remarkable work, *Ethnogénie Gauloise*, was published in the year 1869. In Vol. II., p. 309, the Baron sums up in the following terms his conclusions, arrived at, be it observed, prior to the production of the convincing physical evidence, since discovered in caves, lake-dwellings, and tombs, "nous concluons, que deux types d'une constitution physique aussi différente, que les grands blonds et les petits bruns, ne peuvent être sortis d'une même souche. Il est faux que les hommes à

---

[1] We find for instance the statement that "nineteen-twentieths of the French are descended from Gauls" in Duruy, *History of Rome*, Chap. LIII. p. 83 (English translation). Edited by Prof. Mahaffy.

[2] In references to Strabo, the page of Casaubon's edition will always be given.

tête ronde, qu'on a nommés abusivement les 'Galls,' aient jamais fait partie, ethnologiquement parlant, de la famille celtique..........Il en résulte, que les Celtes ne formèrent jamais en Gaule qu'une minorité dans la population de toutes ces contrées ; qu'ils n'en furent par conséquent pas les premiers habitants ; mais comme l'indiquent leurs propres traditions, conformes à plusieurs données historiques, des conquérants dont la race finit par se perdre, sauf quelques exceptions locales, dans la masse beaucoup plus nombreuse des vaincus."

Startling enough to the ordinary British student, nourished in the traditions of Caesar and Livy, as these conclusions will appear, they seem moderate in comparison with the latest views advanced by the eminent Celtic scholar, M. d'Arbois de Jubainville. For this distinguished member of the Institut goes the length of asserting that there were never in Gallia at any one time more than 60,000 Gauls or Celts (for the terms are synonymous[1]) including non-combatants. In his *Premiers habitants de l'Europe*, Vol. II. p. 7, M. d'Arbois de Jubainville, referring to the observation of Caesar, "nam plebes paene servorum habetur loco," *De Bello Gallico*, VI. 13, expresses himself as follows :

"Elle vivait dans une sorte d'esclavage, quoique la conquête celtique remontât à environ cinq siècles dans la plus grande partie de la Gaule barbare, et que les vaincus eussent probablement presque tous oublié leur langue primitive en apprenant le gaulois, comme plus tard ils oublièrent le gaulois, en apprenant le latin.

"Les membres de l'aristocratie gauloise ne pouvaient pas mettre sous les armes plus de quinze mille cavaliers. Vercingetorix fit cette évaluation d'effectif lors de la grande insurrection dont il fut le chef. Or, une règle de la statistique de ce temps était que le nombre des hommes capables de porter les armes, formait le quart de la population totale.

"Les quinze mille cavaliers, avec leurs femmes, leurs

[1] See p. 5.

enfants et leurs vieux pères formaient donc un total de soixante mille personnes: ainsi une aristocratie, composée de soixante mille âmes, dominait et tenait dans une sorte de servitude le reste de la Gaule barbare, dont le nombre atteignait un peu plus de trois millions."

Had such a paradoxical conclusion as the above been enunciated by a less eminent author than M. d'Arbois de Jubainville, it would have been at once dismissed as undeserving even of consideration. But, whatever adventitious assistance the opinion may derive from the name of the author, it becomes at once evident that, in its exaggerated form, it necessarily falls to the ground when confronted with the plain text of Caesar's Gallic war, and the general consensus of the classical authorities. (From what I gathered during a personal interview with M. d'Arbois de Jubainville, I have reason to hope that he is prepared to modify his extreme views.)

For in Lib. II. c. 4, we find the total of the Belgic contingents alone amounting to 266,000 combatants. In Lib. VII. c. 76, the outside Gallic host brought up for the relief of Alesia, inclusive of Belgae, numbered, according to Caesar, 240,000 infantry and 8000 cavalry[1], while 80,000 more were beleaguered inside with Vercingetorix.

Although M. d'Arbois de Jubainville considers the infantry unworthy of enumeration, as not of Gallic blood, he still does not actually deny that they were present, and draws attention to the fact that the 'plebes,' from which the infantry was presumably recruited, spoke Gallic. It does not appear to strike M. d'Arbois de Jubainville as at all improbable that a minority of 15,000 families should have succeeded in imposing its language on a people numbering three millions.

M. d'Arbois de Jubainville is perhaps not necessarily in conflict with Caesar as to the numbers, only as to the

---

[1] Of the 15,000 cavalry, the number given by M. D'Arbois as estimated by Vercingetorix, only 8000 appear to have obeyed the summons.

nationality of the combatants before Alesia. Whatever its exact composition may have been it is hardly surprising that Caesar described the Gallic-speaking host gathered around Alesia under the general name of 'Galli,' and that he failed to enter into any ethnological subtleties on such an occasion.

That Gallic blood in the Gaul of Caesar's time was confined to the cavalry or fighting aristocracy is a paradox, which—*pace* M. d'Arbois de Jubainville—will not bear serious examination. If we admit that recent discovery proves that the groundwork of the population in western Gaul has always remained Iberian, there must still have been a large admixture of Gauls in the inferior population or "tiers état," which was apparently of no more account in Caesar's day than in France before the Revolution. For we are expressly told by Caesar, Lib. VI. c. 13, that it frequently occurred amongst the Gauls that independent individuals broke down, overburdened with debt or fiscal charges, and losing caste, descended in the social scale to swell the ranks of the poor clients of the nobles.

In the opening chapter of the first book of his Gallic war, is contained the only general reference to distinctions of languages existing in Caesar's Gallia, from which the Rhone valley, formed 60 years earlier into the "Provincia Romana," was excluded. The passage is known to every schoolboy. " All Gaul is divided into three parts, of which the Belgae inhabit one, the Aquitani another, while the people whom we call Galli, but who call themselves Celtae, inhabit the remaining part. All three differ from each other in language, institutions and laws[1]." Although unfortunately Caesar tells us nothing as to the nature of this difference, whether it was of kind, or only of degree,

---

[1] If Caesar had visited Gallia a century or two earlier, he would have found Galli occupying two out of his three divisions. For he expressly states (*De Bell. Gall.* II. 3) that the Belgae, who of old came from beyond the Rhine, expelled Galli then in possession of Belgica.

much light is thrown upon this important point by Strabo.

For in Lib. IV. p. 176, which deals with Gallia, Strabo writes, "Some make a threefold division of it into Aquitani, Belgae and Celtae, of whom the Aquitani differ totally from the other two, both in language and physique, resembling Iberians much more than Gauls. The Belgae and Celtae are both Gauls, to outward appearance, but there is a slight difference of language." We must therefore infer that both Celtae and Belgae spoke Celtic. But as Caesar tells us (L. II. c. 3) that most of the Belgae were sprung from Germans we are led to infer that the Celtic spoken by the Belgae was not as widely different from the German as the two languages became later. When (Lib. I. c. 47) Caesar required to confer with Ariovistus, the negotiations were carried on in Celtic, which the German chief had acquired during his occupation of the country of the Sequani. The difference in language spoken by Celtae and Belgae, referred to both by Caesar and Strabo, is perhaps represented by that between Goidelic and Brythonic later.

With regard to the distribution of the population in ancient Gallia, it seems most probable that what is true of our day was true of Caesar's, viz. that the further you advanced southwards and westwards, the darker and smaller the population became, being further removed from the fair, tall, German type of the north-eastern region, the Belgica of Caesar. That there ever existed anywhere a type of small dark Gauls or Celts is now considered in France a complete delusion.

For the type of Gaul, made known to us by the consensus of classical authorities, was tall, fair and blue-eyed—only differing as Strabo informs us (p. 290) from the German or Teuton in being less fierce, gigantic and ruddy. We read in his life by Suetonius that when Caligula ran short of German prisoners for his sham triumph over that nation, he was obliged to put up with the biggest Gauls he could find. He compelled them to let their hair grow long, dye it red, assume barbarous names and learn German. Again on p. 196, Strabo, comparing Gauls and Germans, writes "they resemble each other in their nature and constitution, and are akin (συγγενεῖς) in blood." Such was the type of the Gauls, who in the year B.C. 390 sacked Rome and are portrayed in Virgil's well-known lines:

> "Aurea caesaries ollis, atque aurea vestis;
> Virgatis lucent sagulis; tum lactea colla
> Auro innectuntur."

Of this type too were the Gauls, who a century later invaded Greece, and pillaged the treasure of Delphi, passing on thence through Macedonia and Thrace into Asia Minor, where they carried fire and sword into its most fertile provinces[1].

These were the centuries when the Gauls were at their prime. But the history of their exploits has been unaccountably neglected by British historians. It is given in full detail and in a most readable form by Amédée Thierry in his *Histoire des Gaulois*.

When Caesar invaded the country, to which they had given their name 'Gallia,' the Gauls were already a degenerate people, as Caesar himself points out. From living remote from the enervating luxuries of the 'Provincia,' and nearer to the Germans, the Belgae alone escaped degeneracy. In *De Bell. Gall.* VI. c. 24, we read, "But there was formerly a time, when the Gauls surpassed the Germans in valour and carried war into their country without provocation."

As a matter of fact it was from Belgica that the Romans mainly derived their knowledge of the Gauls. It was there that Caesar's toughest fighting took place.

[1] The most famous of these Gauls were the Tectosages, who finally settled down in Galatia, and were the ancestors of St Paul's "foolish Galatians."

## INTRODUCTORY.

The adjoining Rhine Provinces, Germania Superior and Inferior, where the tall, fair type of Gallicised Teuton has always predominated, were the only parts of Gallia ever permanently garrisoned by the Romans. The Romans, in the opposite sense, anticipated the Germans in keeping the "Wacht am Rhein." So it is not surprising that, writing about A.D. 350, in the reign of Julian, Ammianus Marcellinus should observe, L. XV. 12, "The Gauls are almost all tall, fair and ruddy, with a terrible gleam in their eyes."

It was not till comparatively late that the Romans had much intercourse with western Gallia, where, in the reign of Gallienus, Bordeaux became an imperial residence.

To Amédée Thierry the anomaly of attributing the small and dark Bretons and Welsh to a Celtic or Cymric stock seems to have presented no difficulty. But the opinion is rapidly gaining ground, both in France and Britain, that in spite of their Cymric name and speech, the population of Brittany and Wales is to be regarded as mainly Iberian. Professor Boyd Dawkins in his *Early Man in Britain* is a strong exponent of this view as regards the Silures, quoting Tacitus[1] to support it.

In those regions of the far west the strain of invading Celts, who imposed their name and language on the conquered indigenous population, has gradually become absorbed and disappeared. As far as language is concerned, the same process has been steadily going on in Ireland, where the descendants of English settlers have become more Irish than the Irish, and yet the English language has prevailed.

While the language has undergone at least two great changes in Ireland, i.e. from Iberian to Celtic and from Celtic to English, the blood in the south and west of the island is probably still mainly Iberian. If the theories of Roger de Belloguet, D'Arbois de Jubainville in France, and Professor Boyd Dawkins in England,

---

[1] *Agricola*, c. 11.

hold good, it will soon be hard to find a purely Celtic race left. In the same chapter where Tacitus refers to the tradition of the Iberian descent of the Welsh Silures, he suggests the likelihood of a German origin of the Caledonians. There is a natural tendency on the part of readers, and especially in the case of countries which they know only by name, to assume that the bulk of the inhabitants belongs to the race which has last given its name to the country. But such assumption frequently turns out to be utterly unfounded. The conquest of a country often involved little more than a change of landlords.

There have from time immemorial been two main classes of invaders, namely that of organized bands of armed adventurers, bringing no women; and that of tribes in search of fresh settlements and consisting of whole families, with all their belongings. If the armed adventurers settled in the conquered country they would intermarry with the native women, and their descendants gradually become merged in the native population which, notwithstanding, would probably have adopted the name and language of their conquerors.

As far as we can gather from the classical authorities the Galli, with the notable exception of the Helvetic emigrants arrested by Caesar, belonged to the first class, and the Germans to the second class of invaders. In the case of the Cimbri and Teutones we know that they moved in huge caravans of covered waggons, as the reader will find further on when I deal with their invasion of Provence.

Of the three races, Iberian, Ligurian and Celtic, found in Gallia Transalpina it appears that Iberians and Ligurians divided between them the possession of the North-Western Mediterranean coast line prior to the appearance of the Celts. For in the *Ora Maritima* of Festus Avienus, which though itself of the 4th century A.D. is based on the *Periplus* of Himilco, the Carthaginian navigator of the 4th century B.C., we find the Rhone assigned as the earliest authentic dividing line between the Iberians and the Ligurians—

> "hujus (sc. Rhodani) alveo
> Ibera tellus atque Ligyes intersecantur"—

and Strabo, p. 166, mentions the former extension of Iberia up to the Rhone.

By the light of recent investigation it indeed appears probable that not only did the mouths of the Rhone separate these two primitive nationalities on the Mediterranean coast, but that in prehistoric times a dividing line between them was carried up northwards into Gallia[1]. Into the midst of this Ibero-Ligurian population, formidable bodies of Gauls or Celts, armed with their then irresistible long swords, began to pour, at dates of which we have no positive record. The contests between Celts and Ligurians are referred to as being of frequent occurrence by Festus Avienus, v. 132 of the *Ora Maritima*:

> "namque Celtarum manu
> Crebrisque dudum proeliis vacuata sunt,
> Liguresque pulsi, ut saepe fors aliquos agit,
> Venere in ista, quae per horrentes tenent
> Plerumque dumos."

While our attention is drawn to encounters between Celts and Ligurians, it is to be observed that nothing is said about any resistance being offered by the Iberians within the limits of Gaul.

Driving a Celtic wedge between Iberians, forced westward, and Ligurians, south-eastward back into the Rhone Valley, the main body of Gauls occupied in force the north-eastern and central plateaus of France, the whole of which they ultimately dominated.

When history opens with Herodotus, about the middle of the fifth century before Christ, we find that bands of Celts had already forced their way right through western Gallia across the Pyrenees, and formed

[1] In Chap. v. this question is more fully treated.

a settlement on the Atlantic sea-board of the Iberian peninsula. But they had not yet reached the Mediterranean. For Herodotus informs us in Lib. II. c. 33, "that the Celts are beyond the Pillars of Hercules," thus locating them somewhere on the coast of the Atlantic Ocean to the extreme west of Europe. While in Lib. VII. c. 165, Herodotus enumerates both Iberians and Ligurians amongst the mercenaries collected from all parts of the Mediterranean by Terillus, the expelled tyrant of Himera, in his final effort to recover his throne, B.C. 480, Celts are conspicuously absent from the list. Inasmuch as in the succeeding centuries—and notably in the first and second Punic Wars in the service of Carthage—the Celts became famous as professional mercenaries, we may consider it proved that in the 5th century B.C. they were as yet unknown to the powers bordering on the Mediterranean.

We must therefore certainly reject Livy's date, B.C. 600, the reign of Tarquinius Priscus, as being at least a century and a half too early for the appearance of Celts in Italy, and it seems doubtful whether his account of the emigration of the two main swarms of Celts under Bellovesus and Sigovesus from a parent hive in France into Italy and Germany respectively will bear serious examination.

In spite of Mommsen's qualified acceptance of the main facts without the date[1], Messrs Alexandre Bertrand and Salomon Reinach, in their recently published joint work *Les Celtes dans la Vallée du Po et du Danube*, go very near to rejecting Livy's narrative altogether. For these exponents of the latest theories on the subject, the Roman Province of Gallia Transalpina was never the parent hive of Celts, of whom there were never enough in the west to have swarmed back over the Western Alps into Italy or Germany.

They argue, too, that if the Cisalpine province had been overrun by Gauls from the Transalpine, we ought

[1] *History of Rome.* English translation. Book II. c. IV.

to find the names of the Bituriges and Arverni figuring there in the place of Insubres and Boii, the latter of whom are scarcely heard of in the Transalpine Province, till we read of them in Caesar's Gallic war, as invading it in conjunction with the Helvetii.

There certainly seems a great deal to be said in favour of the contention that Gallia Cisalpina derived her main contingents of Gauls direct from the valley of the Danube, by which route all authorities are agreed in bringing them originally into Europe. For the Gauls seem to have dropped contingents all along their road through Austria, Germany, and Switzerland to the Rhine, some of whom probably poured over the Rhaetian and Julian Alps into Italy. But the theory of a re-flux of Gauls from Gallia Transalpina is not to be rejected altogether.

The first and only Celtic confederation to establish itself permanently on the Mediterranean sea-board was that of the Volcae. This branch of the Celtic family, from whose name Volcae our word Welsh is derived (as I am reminded by my friend Professor Rhys of Oxford), was the latest to separate itself from the Germans, amongst whom it had found a temporary domicile before crossing the Rhine.

The establishment of the Volcae in the plains between the Rhone and the Pyrenees, occupied previously mainly by an Iberian population, may be fixed approximately at 400 B.C., but nothing is known of the circumstances under which it was effectuated. The Volcae were divided into two branches—Arecomici and Tectosages. The Arecomici, who appear to have been early brought under the civilizing influence of their neighbours the Greeks of Marseilles, were the founders of the great Celtic emporium at Narbonne, which, long before Roman intervention in Gaul, became the principal mart of exchange for native products brought down to the coast from the interior, including tin from Britain.

We learn from Strabo (p. 190) that before the

date of the Roman conquest of Provence (B.C. 122), the over-lordship of the Arverni extended to Narbonne and the Mediterranean sea-board. Thus the Volcae were clients of the Arverni. While, on the right bank of the Rhone, the Celtic confederation of Volcae displaced or enslaved the former Iberian population about B.C. 400, the Ligurian Salyes, or Salluvii, succeeded to the last in barring Celtic access to the Mediterranean on the left bank.

Thus, the country—now known as Provence—lying between the Rhone, the Durance, the Alps and the Mediterranean, although officially regarded by the Romans as part of Gallia Transalpina, was never occupied nor conquered by Gauls. The bulk of the population of this little-known south-eastern corner of France has always remained Ligurian, just as in its south-western corner the Iberians have never been dislodged from Aquitania. To this day, the south-western quarter of France is largely Iberian in its affinities, the Pyrenees having never served as an effectual barrier between races.

This preliminary sketch of the distribution of races in Gallia Transalpina would be incomplete without some mention of the introduction of a Greek element into the population *viâ* Marseilles. If the reader will refer to the section of the Carte de Peutinger reproduced at the end of the volume, he will observe that the name 'Gretia' is given to the region between Marseilles and the Durance.

And first, as regards the foundation of Marseilles, there has been much discussion as to whether the Phocaeans took possession of an existing Phoenician settlement, or whether they were the original founders. The discovery at Marseilles in 1845 of a stone tablet, now preserved in the Museo Borély, engraved with a long Phoenician inscription, embodying minute regulations as to the functions and remuneration of the priests of the god 'Belen' (the sun), was for some time thought to strengthen the argument of those who contended for a pre-existing Phoenician settlement. But it having been ascertained that the stone on which the inscription is engraved is of African origin, it cannot be held to prove anything decisive on the point in dispute.

But besides the stone tablet in question, an altar of Baal and so many images, apparently of Phoenician origin, have come to light, that it is difficult to accept M. Renan's opinion as final against the existence of a previous Phoenician settlement. For how can the discovery of so many Phoenician relics be explained on any other theory than that they were there before the Phocaeans arrived? For in consequence of their bitterly hostile relations it seems very unlikely that Phoenicians or Carthaginians would have ever settled subsequently at Marseilles amongst the Greeks.

For the generally accepted date of 600 B.C., for the original foundation of Marseilles, Timaeus is the definite authority; "They (the Phocaeans) founded it in Liguria one hundred and twenty years, as they say, before the battle of Salamis. Timaeus at least gives this account of its foundation[1]."

We find also in a fragment of Aristotle's lost work (*apud Athenaeum*, XIII. 576) on the Constitution of Marseilles, which he held up to the admiration of the world, the statement, "The Phocaeans who had their trading station in Ionia founded Massilia."

It is however very singular that Herodotus should make no mention whatever of Marseilles, which had existed a century and a half before he wrote his history. As he gives us such a striking narrative of the abandonment of their city by the Phocaeans, in preference to becoming enslaved to the Persians; of their temporary (five years') settlement in Corsica, where they found Phocaeans, who had settled there and founded Alalia

---

[1] *Ps. Scymnus*, 211 ἐν τῇ Λιγυστικῇ δὲ ταύτην ἔκτισαν πρὸ τῆς μάχης τῆς ἐν Σαλαμῖνι γενομένης ἔτεσιν πρότερον ὥς φασιν ἑκατὸν εἴκοσιν. Τιμαῖος οὕτως ἱστορεῖ δὲ τὴν κτίσιν.

twenty years previously; of the sea fight off Alalia, in which 40 out of the 60 Phocaean ships were destroyed by the combined fleet of Carthaginians and Etruscans; of the 20 remaining Phocaean ships abandoning Corsica and founding Hyela (Velia), we should have at least expected some reference to the actual foundation of Marseilles by Phocaeans, which took place half a century before these events.

As long as the Etrusco-Carthaginian naval alliance rendered the power of their combined fleet supreme in the western Mediterranean, there was little chance of the Phocaean Massiliots developing their commerce from Marseilles, which must have had a very modest beginning. But when the Carthaginians suffered temporary collapse by sea and land at the battle of Himera (B.C. 480), which was followed up by the defeat of their confederates, the Etruscans, by the Greeks off Cumae (B.C. 474), the coast was cleared of enemies and the chance came for the rise of the new Phocaean republic in the West.

In the ensuing 70 years, the commerce of Marseilles advanced with surprising rapidity, driving the Carthaginian successors of the Phoenician traders beyond the Pillars of Hercules, and establishing trading stations of its own to the westward at various points along the coast of Gaul and Spain. For the Massiliots do not appear to have directed their energies eastwards at this early period, when their supply of citizens was probably not equal to founding colonies, as they did subsequently at Tauroentum, Olbia, Athenopolis, Antipolis, Nicaea and Monaco.

However, during the fourth century B.C., the Carthaginians succeeded in re-establishing their supremacy at sea, and, this time single-handed (for their allies the Etruscans never got over their catastrophe off Cumae), they cut the Massiliots off from all intercourse with their Spanish emporia, thus recovering all the trade they had lost.

Had not the Romans, who from the first had been warm allies of the Massiliots, come eventually to their rescue, it might have been all over with the fortunes of Marseilles. But realizing at the outbreak of the first Punic War the necessity of becoming a first-rate naval power, the Romans threw such energy into ship-building, as, before its close, to disable the Carthaginian navy and wrest from their rival once for all the command of the western basin of the Mediterranean.

Thus it was owing to the Romans that Marseilles recovered the commercial prosperity which she has enjoyed almost uninterruptedly ever since. As an indication of the intimate relations existing in early times between Rome and Marseilles we read that the tenth part of the spoil of Veii, dedicated to the Delphic Apollo by Camillus, was deposited in the Massiliot treasury at Delphi. It is also related that a collection was made at Marseilles at the time of the capture and burning of Rome by the Gauls, for the sufferers by the fire[1]. In return for this generosity, places of honour were always reserved for the Massiliots at public games at Rome.

But it was especially during the Punic wars that Marseilles and Rome rendered each other invaluable services, their interests being identical.

---

[1] We may compare here the efforts made by the commercial cities of the Aegean to assist Rhodes after the earthquake, in the time of the Ptolemies: Marseilles, in fact, was in the North-west of the Mediterranean a charitable agency similar to Alexandria in the south. It is interesting to find that the wealth of commercial centres contributed in the earliest times to alleviate international, as well as domestic, calamities. So after all the Lord Mayor's fund is no new institution.

## CHAPTER II.

### Hannibal in the Rhone Valley.

The first important event in Roman history, coming within the scope of this work, of which any details have been handed down to us is Hannibal's invasion of Italy. It was this event which for the first time brought a Roman army into the Rhone valley (B.C. 218). On the outbreak of the second Punic War, which they had just declared against Carthage, the Romans hoped, by despatching armies by sea to operate in Sicily and Spain, that they might succeed in keeping the war out of Italy. The Consuls of the year were Tiberius Sempronius and Publius Cornelius Scipio. To the former Sicily was assigned as his province, with instructions to carry the war into Africa, if circumstances seemed to require it. Spain fell to the lot of Scipio.

When the Carthaginians had lost their supremacy at sea and with it all hold of Sicily and Sardinia, as the result of their defeat by the Romans in the first Punic War, they determined to seek compensation for this blow by extending their influence and consolidating their power in Spain. Although the Romans clearly perceived that an enormous increase of strength must inevitably accrue to the Carthaginians, from acquiring Spain as a new field for recruiting their armies, they were powerless to interfere, being fully engaged nearer home in a life and death contest with the Cisalpine Gauls on their flank. Thus Spain became the Carthaginian base at the outset of the second Punic War.

His colleague Sempronius having duly set out with his fleet and army for Sicily in the spring of the year B.C. 218, Scipio was about to embark for Spain, when news arrived of the critical state of affairs in Cisalpine Gaul. For the origin of the wars waged intermittently with the Cisalpine Gauls by the Romans for two centuries before their final subjugation in B.C. 191, we must go back to the sack and burning of Rome, B.C. 390—a disaster brought about accidentally by the wanton interference of Romans in the struggle between the Gauls and Etruscans.

For having, about 20 years before, driven the Etruscans from the Po valley out of all but a few exceptionally strong places, such as Mantua, inaccessible from its surrounding marshes, the Cisalpine Gauls, their numbers constantly swollen by fresh swarms of their Transalpine kinsmen, had overflowed first into Umbria, and thence through the passes of the Apennines into Etruria proper.

They might have stopped short of attacking Rome, had the Roman ambassadors abstained from joining in the hostilities before Clusium. But once blood was shed between Romans and Gauls, it was destined to flow in a never-ending stream. Sometimes against the Cisalpine Gauls single-handed, at others against Cisalpines banded with Etrurians or Samnites, and sometimes in alliance with Transalpine Gaesatae, or mercenaries, the Romans waged bloody wars with fluctuating success between B.C. 390 and the final subjugation of the Boii by Scipio Nasica B.C. 191.

The defeat of the Romans 390 B.C. at the battle of the Allia, followed by the sack and burning of Rome by the Gauls, had been a rude beginning of relations between the Eternal City and the Gallic tribes. It was a lesson, which was branded deep into the flesh of Romans. As long as the Republic lasted, there was an ever present sense in Roman breasts of overwhelming danger in the background from Gallic invasion. The subjugation of Gallia Cisalpina and its constitution B.C. 191 as a Roman province by no means put an end to their fears. For what the Romans really dreaded was the vague limitless 'Gaul' outside and wrapping round Gallia Cisalpina—itself a mere reservoir fed by the vast ocean of barbarians always ready to flow over the Alps into Italy. This Gaul beyond the Alps must by no means be confined to the Roman Province Gallia Transalpina, answering to modern France. To be rightly understood, it must be conceived of as including all the countries separated from Italy by the whole semicircle of the Alps. Other wars waged by the Romans were wars, but Gallic wars were declared 'tumultus,' which required military service of old and young. A special fund was always in reserve in the Treasury to meet the expense of Gallic irruptions—a fund which was scrupulously respected and left untouched till Julius Caesar seized it at the close of his conquest of Gaul on the ground that his victories had put an end to further danger from that quarter.

To exterminate the Senones, the nearest of Gallic settlers to Roman territory, and wipe out the insult of the burning of Rome, required a hundred years of intermittent fighting. It was not till B.C. 283 that the first Roman colony—Sena Gallica on the coast of the Adriatic—was founded on soil won back from Gallic invaders of Italy.

It was next the turn of the gallant Boii, and their allies the Insubres, to encounter the Roman arms. The first period of the war against these tribes had lasted about 60 years, when, despairing of holding out longer, after their chief centre Mediolanum (Milan) had fallen into the hands of the Romans, the Boii and Insubres sued for peace, giving hostages as a guarantee of abstention from further hostilities. As the territory of these two tribes was the most fertile and central of Cisalpine Gaul, the Romans determined to plant at Placentia on the south bank of the Po, and at Cremona a few miles to the north of that river, strong military colonies, which should hold the Gauls in check.

Hardly were the hostages handed over, and peace concluded, when emissaries from Hannibal arrived to announce his projected invasion, and excite the Gauls of the Cisalpine to fresh insurrection. Without hesitation, the Gauls, responding to Hannibal's summons, threw themselves in overwhelming numbers on the three Roman commissioners, engaged in the act of parcelling out the confiscated Gallic territory amongst the newly arrived colonists, 6,000 of whom were destined to occupy Placentia, and 6,000 Cremona[1].

Of neither of these places were the defences sufficiently completed to offer adequate protection to the colonists, who were taken completely by surprise. The sight of these chains forging for their future subjection excited the Gauls to such a degree, that they drove the commissioners and colonists clean off the ground; they fled for their lives as far as Mutina (Modena), where they at last found shelter.

To aid in rescuing the beleaguered commissioners, and in re-establishing Roman authority in Cisalpine Gaul, the consul Publius Cornelius Scipio found himself under the necessity of detaching under the praetor Atilius one of the two legions with which he was about to start for Spain. It was clear that the Romans had got a Gallic, as well as a Carthaginian, war on hand. If the two should combine, and the Gauls find in Hannibal a leader capable of welding their forces into a solid mass, the outlook for the Romans would be desperate. It was more than ever urgent to keep Hannibal out of Italy.

However, to raise a new legion was a work of time, and the summer was well advanced, when at last Scipio got under way with his flotilla of sixty quinquiremes, conveying 8,000 Roman and 14,000 allied infantry, with 600 Roman and 1,600 allied cavalry. Of Scipio's voyage

[1] Polyb. III. 40.

## CHAP. II.

we read in Polybius (I quote from Mr Shuckburgh's translation), "Publius Cornelius Scipio coasted along Liguria, and crossing in five days from Pisae to Marseilles, dropped anchor at the most eastern mouth of the Rhone, called the mouth of Marseilles, and began disembarking his troops[1]." From Livy we learn that during the latter part of the voyage the Roman flotilla sailed past the mountains of the Salyes (Salluvii), and that the sea being rough, the troops were on their arrival incapacitated by sea-sickness for immediate operations[2].

From the classical narratives, one would be inclined to infer that Marseilles was situated at the mouth of the Rhone[3]. As a matter of fact, that city lies at least twenty miles to the eastward of its most easterly branch, and is completely separated from the Rhone by the Étang de Berre, a vast salt-water lake, and by several ranges of limestone hills. Along the foot of the hills which shut in the city of Marseilles on the north there intervenes a sheltered undercliff some five miles in width, forming a picturesque approach to the sea, in pleasing contrast to the bare plateau traversed to the north of the range. To cultivate and at the same time garrison this fertile band of territory, the Phocaean traders took into their service friendly Celts, who served as a convenient buffer between them and their persistent assailants the Ligurian Salyes. The city itself was originally confined to the peninsula to the west of its almost land-locked harbour, which was unconnected with any fresh-water inlet.

In selecting this site for their city, the Phocaeans shewed the greatest sagacity. For every Mediterranean river-mouth gets sooner or later silted up and rendered useless as a harbour. Such is notably the case with the

---

[1] Polyb. III. 41.
[2] Livy XXI. 26. The mountains of the Salluvii are now called 'Les Maures,' extending from Hyères to the valley of the Argens.
[3] See Maps of Bouches du Rhône and Plan of ancient Marseilles.

Rhone, the navigation of which even in the days of Caius Marius was so difficult, that that commander, while awaiting the invasion of the Cimbri and Teutones, had to cut a separate channel, by which to convey supplies from the sea to his camp on Les Alpines—a jagged and picturesque range of hills cutting the Rhone valley at a right angle near Tarascon.

Considering the friendly relations existing between the Romans and Massiliots, it was only natural that Scipio should call at Marseilles on his way to Spain, with the view of getting news of Hannibal's latest movements. Being in constant communication by means of swift despatch boats with their important trading station Emporia, at the foot of the Pyrenees, the Massiliots were well posted in the proceedings of the Carthaginians in that quarter.

Great was the astonishment and disappointment of Scipio, when he learned from the friendly Massiliots that their common enemy Hannibal, whom Scipio still fondly hoped to encounter in Spain, had not only crossed the Pyrenees, but had already reached the Rhone. This must have happened about the end of July or early in August.

Upon receiving this intelligence, Scipio at once despatched up the Rhone valley a cavalry reconnaissance, consisting of 300 legionary horsemen with some of the friendly Celts[1] in the pay of the Massiliots as guides, with orders to find out the exact whereabouts of the Carthaginian army. For Scipio did not yet despair of co-operating with the Volcae in effectually opposing Hannibal's passage of the Rhone.

But the Carthaginian general had again been too quick for the Romans. For after his descent from the Pyrenees on Illiberis, Hannibal, by means of bribes and persuasion, was so successful in winning over the Gallic kinglets ('reguli') assembled at Ruscino (Roussillon),

[1] Probably the Albici referred to in Caesar's *De Bello Civili*, I. c. 34, inhabitants of the modern city of Riez, Dept. Basses Alpes.

that they not only allowed him to pass unmolested, but supplied him with timber for the construction of rafts and canoes for the transport of his forces across the Rhone[1]. However, at the actual point of his crossing, Roquemaure, on a level with Orange, four days' march from the sea (so arranged as to take him above the junction of, and avoid the difficult passage of, the Durance at Avignon), Hannibal ultimately found himself opposed by some Volcae, who at that period appear to have occupied territory on the left bank of the Rhone, opposite their main settlements on the right bank.

To overcome this show of opposition to his passage of the Rhone in front, Hannibal sent round a party, chiefly consisting of Spaniards under Hanno, to a point higher up the river, where a large island facilitated the passage. Having crossed successfully, the Spaniards floating over on their clothes stretched on bladders, Hanno, descending the left bank, threw the ranks of the Volcae into confusion by setting fire to the camp in their rear. So Hannibal effected his passage practically unopposed, the 37 elephants being got over last.

While the somewhat tedious operation of conveying the elephants over was in progress, Hannibal, who had meanwhile been informed of the disembarcation of Scipio's army at the Massiliot mouth of the Rhone, despatched a body of 500 Numidian horsemen to reconnoitre the enemy. So completely was the Numidian rider at one with his horse, that he used no bridle to guide him. Falling in with the cavalry sent forward by Scipio, the Numidians attacked them with their usual impetuosity. A desperate mêlée ensued, in which about 200 were slain on either side. But the Romans eventually got the better of it, and drove the Numidians back to the Carthaginian camp. This was the first Roman blood shed in Transalpine Gaul.

While Hannibal hesitated between accepting the

[1] Polyb. III. 42.

battle which Scipio was anxious to force upon him and continuing his march direct to the Alps, Magalus, one of their chiefs, and other envoys of the Cisalpine Boii, arrived in camp in the nick of time, offering themselves as guides, and protesting their readiness to share the risks of the passage. As the envoys of the Boii had themselves just crossed the Alps, their presence was the best proof which could be offered to the hesitating Carthaginians of the feasibility of the passage. The Boii, being in the habit of getting over Gaesatae or Transalpine mercenaries to assist them in their wars with the Romans, naturally made light of the difficulties of the Alps. Yielding to these representations, the Carthaginians broke up their camp, pitched at the point, four days' march from the sea, where the crossing of the Rhone had been effected. In four more days they reached the junction of the Rhone and the Isère, forming the fertile island described by Polybius[1], making together eight days' march.

From the present distance of about 120 miles from the mouth of the Rhone to the so-called island at its junction with the Isère, we must deduct at least eight to allow for the alluvial deposit brought down by the Rhone in 2000 years. This would leave 112 miles, which at the rate of 14 miles a day would just require eight days to accomplish. The four days' march of 56 miles from the sea would thus agree with fixing the site of Hannibal's passage of the Rhone at the village of Roquemaure, on a level with Orange.

The first day's march from Orange northwards lying across a level plain, the Carthaginians would have encountered no serious obstacle, as the channels of the not-unfrequent torrents would have been dry in the late summer. As it was now Hannibal's immediate object to avoid an encounter with the Romans, he doubtless availed himself of the favourable nature of the ground to put as great a distance as possible between himself

[1] Polyb. III. 39.

and Scipio by exceeding his average marching-distance on the first day.

It is therefore probable that he pushed on as far as Donzère, some twenty miles north of Orange, where the wide plain of Provence suddenly ceases, and the Rhone enters the first of the narrow gorges which recur at intervals for the rest of its course. It is at Donzère, where a picturesque line of mediaeval towers and fortifications now crowns the heights commanding the entrance of the gorge, that the brightness of the Midi ends, or begins, according to the direction in which the traveller is proceeding.

As one surveys the almost limitless plain stretching southward, and presenting quite oriental features, one realizes how completely the white burnooses of the Numidians, the turbans of the Africans, and the line of the elephants must have harmonized with the landscape. One reflects too that if Hannibal had meant fighting, the plain was his opportunity with his vast superiority of cavalry. But he knew how much depended on his getting safely over the Alps before the weather broke up, and wisely determined to allow nothing to detain him on the lower Rhone. Had he adhered to this prudent resolution, instead of wasting precious weeks in the country of the Allobroges, Hannibal would have avoided the loss of half his army in crossing the Alps.

Once the gorge of Donzère was entered, the marching must have become more difficult and the rate slower. The second camping ground was probably Montelimar, and the third the junction of the Drôme with the Rhone, between Livron and Loriol. That no mention is made of even so considerable a river as the Drôme, shows how meagre was the information about the local geography possessed either by Polybius or Livy. The fourth day's march brought Hannibal to the junction of the Isère with the Rhone—the only point we can determine with absolute certainty on the whole march.

On the third day after Hannibal had quitted it, Scipio arrived in order of battle at the deserted Carthaginian camp on the Rhone opposite Roquemaure. Recognizing the hopelessness of overtaking the enemy, the Roman commander at once decided to march back to the mouth of the Rhone. There he immediately re-embarked his army, which he despatched to Spain under his brother Cnaeus, realizing the importance of cutting Hannibal off from his base in that country. Retaining but a handful of followers, Publius Scipio himself sailed back to Genoa, purposing to take over from the praetors Manlius and Atilius the legions under their orders in Cisalpine Gaul. It was Scipio's intention to be ready with these troops to oppose Hannibal on his descent from the Alps into the Po valley.

## CHAPTER III.

### HANNIBAL'S PASSAGE OF THE ALPS.

THAT it is still an open question, and one which will probably never be cleared up, by what pass Hannibal actually crossed the Alps, is mainly due to the incompetence of Polybius as a geographer and to his almost total suppression of names, in spite of his undertaking to make them intelligible to his readers[1].

Instead of invaluable local names, Polybius proceeds to offer to his readers an irrelevant dissertation on the celestial and terrestrial globes[2].

When he descends to particulars he writes, "The Rhone rises to the north-west of the Adriatic Gulf[3]," and goes on to describe the ridges of the Alps, as "beginning at Marseilles and extending up to the head of the Adriatic," concluding as follows—"I speak with confidence on these points, because I have questioned persons actually engaged on the facts, and have inspected the country and gone over the Alpine pass myself, in order to inform myself of the truth and see with my own eyes[4]."

Of Hannibal's passage of the Isère, a deep and considerable river at its junction with the Rhone near Valence, we are not told a word. Yet, in order to act as arbitrator between the rival claims of the two brothers to the principacy of the Allobroges inhabiting

[1] Polyb. III. 36.   [2] Polyb. III. 36, 37.
[3] Polyb. III. 47.   [4] Polyb. III. 48.

the 'insula,' to the north of that river, we must infer that he did cross it.

We are however told by Polybius[1] that, after arriving at the junction of the Rhone and the Isère, the Carthaginians continued to march for ten days by the side of "*the* river"—a distance of 800 stades (100 miles). Read in conjunction with a previous passage[2] we must conclude that the Rhone is the river intended by Polybius. Yet a march of 100 miles by that river would have carried Hannibal 40 miles beyond Lyons, quite out of his way to the north without bringing him to the foot of the Alps. No known writer has been bold or consistent enough to follow the text of Polybius in adopting such an improbable course. The truth seems to be that Polybius was mistaken in his river, but right as to distance. For a march of 100 miles up the Isère would have just brought Hannibal to the foot of the Alps and the beginning of his difficulties. He would, too, in this case have been marching in the right direction, viz. east, towards the Alps and Italy. I am therefore decidedly of opinion that the river followed from the junction was the Isère and not the Rhone.

By making Hannibal follow the course of the Isère for a hundred miles eastwards, I do not commit myself definitely to a continuous march either on the right or left bank of that river. It is sufficient for my argument to show that the main body of the Carthaginian army followed the course of the Isère for 100 Roman miles, *i.e.* as far as its junction with the Arc near St Pierre d'Albigny, where the Mont Cenis Railway branches from the Isère Valley to reach the Alps by the valley of the Arc. I believe that Hannibal followed precisely the same course.

In drawing attention to the fact that St Pierre d'Albigny is just 100 miles from the island of Polybius, and precisely on the direct road to Turin where Hannibal is first heard of, on emerging from the Alps, I think

---

[1] Polyb. III. 50.  [2] Polyb. III. 39.

CHAP. III.                                29

I may fairly claim to have rendered it more probable that the Isère was the river followed by Hannibal than the Rhone.

That Hannibal with the bulk of his army crossed to the northern or right bank of the Isère and passed some time in the above mentioned fertile island, must be admitted as most probable. For the arbitration between the conflicting claims of the two princes and the supplying to Hannibal's army a fresh outfit of arms, clothes and boots by the elder brother Brancus in return for the decision in his favour, could hardly have been conducted outside the limits of the country of the Allobroges.

When, on the completion of these operations, the Carthaginian army was again set in motion, it was conducted by the adherents of Brancus across the plains towards the Alps, and probably recrossed the Isère to its left bank near Grenoble. It was probably the heights, which command that city, which were found in the hostile occupation of the unfriendly section of the Allobroges, which sided with the younger brother.

It being impossible to arrive at absolute certainty as to the actual pass by which Hannibal crossed the Alps, we shall perhaps get nearest the truth by striking a balance between the accounts, given by Polybius and Livy respectively, rejecting those statements in each, which are irreconcileable with topographical requirements, of which they were both very ill informed.

Guided by these considerations, it becomes necessary in my opinion to reject that part of Livy's itinerary, by which Hannibal is made to double back unnecessarily at least four days' march to the south to the Durance: the difficulties of the passage of which shifting river are so graphically described by the Latin historian.

For it was the foreknowledge of and the desire to avoid these very difficulties which originally determined Hannibal to cross the Rhone at Roquemaure above Avignon, just below which city the Durance effects its junction with that river. He would otherwise have crossed lower down at the "Trajectus Rhodani[1]"—between Arles and Avignon—where from the earliest times travellers between Spain and Italy were ferried over the Rhone and where, in our own day, travellers branch from the main P.L.M. line for Spain. It seems then hard to believe, that once in the valley of the Isère, four days' march to the northward of the Durance, Hannibal would have wantonly re-traced his steps so far southwards, this time across the intricate and barren spurs of the Department of the Basses Alpes.

For rejecting Livy's deflection of Hannibal's march to the southward and passage of the Durance, we are supported by the authority of Mommsen, who carries Hannibal up the Rhone valley towards Lyons, as far as Vienne, and thence across the plains of the Allobroges to the Mont du Chat, bringing him down by an abrupt descent upon the Lac du Bourget.

While I agree with Mommsen in rejecting Livy's narrative, I disagree entirely with him in bringing Hannibal quite out of his way up into a narrow trap between a bend of the Rhone and the Lac du Bourget, when it was open to him to get back into the Isère Valley over an easy col now utilized by the Lyons-Grenoble railway.

That at St Pierre d'Albigny, a little above Montmelian, Hannibal quitted the Isère for the Arc valley seems on the whole most probable. This, as I have already observed, is the course followed by the Mt Cenis railway, and is the direct line over the Alps from the country of the Allobroges to that of the Taurini, amongst whom, according to both Livy[2] and Polybius[3], Hannibal descended. Had Hannibal continued to follow the Isère to its source and crossed the Little

---

[1] See map, p. 12.
[2] Livy XXI. 38. "The tribe that he first encountered on his descent into Italy were the Taurini" (Church and Brodribb's Translation).
[3] Polybius, quoted by Strabo, p. 209.

St Bernard, he must have descended on Aosta, the country of the Salassi. It was over the Little St Bernard that the first carriage road was constructed over the Alps.

Those authors who adopt the Pass of the Mt Genèvre ignore the fact that Pompey, who first opened up that pass on his road to Spain, expressly states in his letter to the Senate to be found in Sallust (*Bellum Jugurthinum*, Teubner edition, appendix) that it was not the route followed by Hannibal.

While for the general topographical reasons stated above, I incline on the whole to accept one or other of the Mt Cenis passes, as that crossed by Hannibal, I cannot shut my eyes to the strong claims of the Col de l'Argentière, if the question is to be decided by the authority of texts alone.

If Livy is to be mainly relied upon, I consider that his narrative, of which the passage of the Durance forms a striking feature, fits in with the Col de l'Argentière much better than with the Mt Genèvre. For had the Mt Genèvre been the pass intended by Livy, there would have been no occasion to cross the Durance at all. For on striking the Durance valley, after surmounting the pass separating it from that of the Drac, Hannibal would have naturally marched up the right bank of the Durance to its source in the Mt Genèvre. Whereas he must have crossed it (as described by Livy), to get to the Col de l'Argentière.

I admit that, as Mr Douglas Freshfield forcibly shows in his *Alpine Pass of Hannibal*[1], one must either reject the evidence of Varro or accept the Col de l'Argentière. For in the enumeration of the five passes[2] known to the Romans of his day (*i.e.* the latter years of the republic), Varro's No. 2 can refer to no other than the Col de l'Argentière. On the other hand No. 2 in the order of the four passes named by Polybius[3], of

[1] *Proceedings of the Royal Geographical Society*, October No. 1886.
[2] Preserved by Servius on *Virg. Aen.* x. p. 13.
[3] Quoted by Strabo, p. 209.

which Mr Freshfield makes no mention, expressly specifies the descent of Hannibal on Turin, and therefore cannot apply to the Col de l'Argentière, which leads by the valley of the Stura to Cuneo—fifty-five miles south of Turin.

In order to assist the reader to understand the whole question, I subjoin the two lists of the western passes of the Alps used by the Romans, with their modern names.

FIVE PASSES OF VARRO.   FOUR PASSES OF POLYBIUS.

(In both lists the numbering is from South to North.)

(1) Una quae est juxta mare per Ligures.
(Cornice or Alpes Maritimes. Turbia pass.)

(2) Altera qua Hannibal transiit.
(Col del'Argentière. Ubaye-Stura valleys.)

(3) Tertia qua Pompeius ad Hispaniense bellum profectus est.
(Mont Genèvre. Durance-Doria Riparia valleys.)

(4) Quarta, qua Hasdrubal de Gallia in Italiam venit. (Mt Cenis.)

(5) Quinta quae quondam a Graecis possessa est.
(Petit St Bernard and Val d'Aoste (Doria Baltea).)[1]

(α) διὰ Λιγύων μὲν τὴν ἔγγιστα τῷ Τυρρηνικῷ πελάγει.
(Cornice or Alpes Maritimes. Turbia pass.)

(β) εἶτα τὴν διὰ Ταυρίνων (Turin) ἣν 'Αννίβας διῆλθεν.
(Mt Cenis or Mont Genèvre.)

(γ) εἶτα τὴν διὰ Σαλάσσων.
(Petit St Bernard and the Val d'Aoste.)

(δ) εἶτα τὴν διὰ 'Ραιτῶν.
(Brenner.)

To Livy, who wrote in the reign of Augustus, more than a century after Polybius, from whom he borrowed the main features of his narrative, though he diverged from him so widely in bringing Hannibal down to the Durance, we are indebted for the few invaluable names preserved in connection with Hannibal's march from the Pyrenees to the Alps. It is in Livy that we find recorded the names of the townships Illiberis, Ruscino,

---

[1] The modern name Aosta is derived from the ancient Augusta Praetoria,—so called from the fact that Augustus made it a station of his Praetorian cohorts. The Salassi—the inhabitants of the Val d'Aoste—paid the penalty for having stolen the Emperor's baggage by being sold as slaves.

and of the tribes of the Volcae, Tricastini, Vocontii, and Tricorii. But it is strange that no mention should be made of the important confederation of the Cavari, occupying the left bank of the Rhone above the Durance, through whose territory lay Hannibal's four days' march from the passage of the Rhone to its junction with the Isère[1].

Neither the Greek nor the Latin historian attempts any description of the physical features of the Rhone valley, nor enlivens his narrative by any reference to the mode of life, or degree of civilization attained by the natives. We get no general information, such as Herodotus, Caesar, or Strabo would have afforded. We are left completely in the dark as to the existence of any native settlements at Nîmes, Arles, Avignon or Vienne, though all those places must have been of considerable importance. Of the latter place, as the chief settlement of the Allobroges, and presumably the depot whence were drawn the arms and clothes supplied by Brancus to Hannibal, we should at least have expected some mention. To have sufficed to fit out 50,000 infantry and 12,000 cavalry, of which Hannibal's army in the Rhone valley consisted, the factories of the Allobroges must have been very extensive.

Although we get no precise information on the point from either Polybius or Livy, it seems certain that Hannibal must have been considerably delayed in the country of the Allobroges by the business of arbitrating between the contending brothers and of refitting his army. He paid dearly for this expenditure of precious time. For his passage of the Alps, which a month earlier would have been accomplished with comparative ease, as far as the elements were concerned, proved from the break-up of the weather so disastrous, that more than half his army perished.

[1] The Cavari occupied riparian territory on the E. of the Rhone, between the Isère and the Durance, while the Ligurian Vocontii occupied a parallel zone across the spurs of the Alps.

Of the 50,000 infantry and 12,000 cavalry with which Hannibal approached the Alps, only 20,000 infantry (viz. 12,000 Africans and 8000 Spaniards) and 6000 cavalry survived to reach Italy. As, partly owing to the supineness of the Carthaginian Government, partly to the Roman superiority at sea, Hannibal appears to have received no reinforcements either from Spain or Africa till after the battle of Cannae, two years later, (B.C. 216), it is certain that the bulk of the so-called Carthaginian armies with which he gained his greatest victories over the Romans consisted of Gauls and Ligurians. At Cannae alone Hannibal's losses consisted of 4000 of the latter to only 1500 Spaniards and Africans[1].

In spite, however, of the warmth of their invitation to Hannibal to come amongst them and the protestations of their readiness to flock to his standard, the Cisalpine Gauls at first held aloof, probably deterred by the presence of the superior forces of the Romans. The cavalry encounter near the river Ticinus, to which the narrow escape of the consul Publius Scipio, badly wounded in the affray and rescued by the gallantry of his son, the future Scipio Africanus, lent its chief importance, was not in itself decisive enough to change the attitude of the Gauls. But, after the victory of the Carthaginians at the Trebia, to which the desertion of a Gallic contingent serving under the Romans largely contributed, the ever-dwindling force of Hannibal was recruited by sixty thousand Gauls and Ligurians. With this swollen army, in defiance of the season—it was the depth of winter—Hannibal pushed on up the valley of the Trebia into the heart of the Apennines, hoping to descend upon Etruria by the valley of the Magra, and to excite that province to revolt against the Romans. But the violence of the wind and the intensity of the cold exceeding even his Alpine experiences, compelled him to desist and retrace his steps down the Trebia to

[1] Polyb. III. 117.

within ten miles of Placentia, where the Roman legions were recovering from their recent defeat.

In spite of their sorry plight, the Carthaginians on the following day offered battle, which was again readily accepted by the consul Sempronius—the same commander whose rashness had occasioned the defeat of the Trebia.

On this occasion, however, the fighting, which was exceptionally desperate at the outset, was prematurely put a stop to by nightfall, and led to no decisive result. Failing in his attempt to get possession of Placentia, Hannibal withdrew into Liguria (whether the Liguria to the north or south of the Apennines is not expressly stated), where he passed the remainder of his first winter in Italy[1].

Having followed Hannibal from the foot of the Pyrenees into Liguria, we must take leave of him there in the late winter of B.C. 218 or the early spring of 217.

[1] Livy, XXI. 59.

## CHAPTER IV.

### INVASIONS OF CISALPINE GAUL AND LIGURIA BY HASDRUBAL AND MAGO.

FOR the next ten years of the second Punic War, B.C. 217—208, during which the Romans were actively engaged with Hannibal in central and southern Italy, nothing of importance occurred in the regions within the range of this work. But the spring of B.C. 207 is notable for the rapid march of Hasdrubal from Spain through the western passes of the Pyrenees into Gaul, and across the Rhone valley to the Alps. On this occasion, not only did the Gauls, as Livy tells us[1], everywhere receive him favourably, but contingents of the powerful Arverni and other tribes followed him into Italy.

The Alpine nations too, who had given Hannibal so much trouble, allowed Hasdrubal to pass unmolested, realizing by this time that the Carthaginians only wanted a road through the Alps by the passage which Hannibal had opened up, probably over the Mont Cenis. For the Durance valley route, as I explained in the preceding chapter, leading over the Mont Genèvre pass from the lower Rhone valley, lay much too far south to have ever served as a convenient passage from central Gaul into Italy.

When the news of Hasdrubal's unexpected arrival in the valley of the Po, and of a contingent of 8000 Ligurians being prepared to join him, was sent to Rome by L. Porcius, the praetor, who commanded a weak

[1] Livy, XXVII. 39.

CHAP. IV. 37

force in Cisalpine Gaul, the greatest consternation prevailed. If the junction between Hasdrubal and Hannibal could only be effected, the Romans, barely able to hold their ground against Hannibal alone, must inevitably be crushed.

If Hasdrubal had only pushed on at once, there was nothing to have stopped him from joining his brother. But his evil star drove him to waste the precious time gained by his rapid march, in laying siege to the now impregnable fortress of Placentia, which, even with its incomplete defences, had defied Hannibal ten years earlier. It was this delay which enabled the consul Claudius Nero, who commanded against Hannibal in southern Italy, to form and carry out the daring conception of rapidly transporting 7000 of his picked troops to reinforce his plebeian colleague Livius, who with an inadequate force was fearfully awaiting Hasdrubal's advance in Umbria. It was the crushing defeat of Hasdrubal at the battle of the river Metaurus, resulting from this brilliant manœuvre, which practically decided the second Punic War in favour of the Romans. However, in the summer of B.C. 205, two years after the defeat and death of Hasdrubal, while Hannibal still held on to the Lacinian promontory in Bruttii, the Carthaginians determined to make one more attempt to create a diversion in Liguria by exciting a rising of Ligurians and Gauls.

This time it was to be the turn of the youngest brother Mago to try his hand at retrieving the failing fortunes of Hannibal. Thrice, in the first year of the war, had Mago distinguished himself by his daring. First, after the cavalry engagement on the Ticino, where Publius Scipio was wounded and driven back, it was Mago who had swum the Po with his Numidians in pursuit of the retreating enemy; at the Trebia, it was he who decided the battle by rising in the rear of the Romans from ambush, and throwing them into confusion ; and it was Mago to whom Hannibal confided the hard task of keeping the Gallic contingent up to the mark in the trying march through the Etruscan marshes, which cost Hannibal the loss of an eye.

Sailing from the island of Minorca, where he had passed the winter, with 30 war-ships and a fleet of transports conveying 12,000 infantry, 2000 cavalry, and a number of elephants, Mago made a sudden descent on Genoa, which he captured without striking a blow[1]. However, not feeling strong enough to retain possession of so important a place—for, like Marseilles, Genoa was in intimate alliance with Rome, and used as a friendly port by the Romans—he set fire to the town and withdrew with his rich booty to Savona, where he deposited it in the custody of his allies, the Ligures Alpini.

At this time the Ligurians of the Western Riviera were engaged in internecine warfare. The lowland Ingauni—a comparatively civilized tribe occupying the coast at Albenga, were at war with the Epanterii—a highland people dwelling among the Ligurian Alps. By making an alliance with the Ingauni Mago secured at once a footing on the coast and access to the pass over the Apennines by the valley of the Centa, which falls into the sea at Albenga. His first step was doubtless to seize the rocky island of Gallinara, which lies like a guardship off the shore.

Occupying the widest and most fertile plain to be met with on the whole Riviera, the Ingauni could always supply the necessaries of life to coasting navigation, and were brought earlier into contact with traders than their less fortunate neighbours. It was for this reason that Mago selected Albenga for the base of his operations, reckoning on finding there abundance of corn, fresh food, and forage, of which his men and beasts must have stood in urgent need after their long sea voyage.

Joining in a successful attack on the Epanterii Montani, Mago got his share of the prisoners captured, whom he at once despatched to Carthage with the plunder secured at Genoa, being anxious to lose no time

---

[1] Livy, XXVIII. 46.

in sending home proof of the success of his expedition. Unluckily, however, for him, 80 of his merchantmen were made prizes by the Roman admiral, Cnaeus Octavius, who kept a sharp look-out from his station off the island of Sardinia.

While Mago still lay with his fleet off Albenga he received direct from Carthage a reinforcement of ships and men, which contrived to escape the vigilance of the Roman admiral. On the strength of this accession of strength, the Carthaginian general at once summoned a council of the chiefs of the Gauls and Ligurians, of both of which nationalities an immense host had flocked into Albenga[1].

Addressing the assembled chiefs, and pointing to the ships just arrived from Carthage, as a proof of the determination of his government to assist them to the utmost of its power in attaining their independence of the Romans, Mago strongly urged the immediate enrolment of the largest possible force of Gauls and Ligurians.

To this appeal, however, neither Gauls nor Ligurians responded with much alacrity. While both nationalities professed willingness to assist, the Gauls begged to be allowed to aid secretly in supplying stores, while the Ligurians asked for two months' delay before enlisting fresh soldiers.

It must have soon become clear to Mago that neither Gauls nor Ligurians were as ripe for revolt or as ready to take up arms as the Carthaginian government had reckoned on. Having astutely availed themselves of Mago's assistance in their campaign against their highland enemies the Epanterii, the Ingauni considered that they had had enough of fighting for that year (B.C. 205).

Like their neighbours the Gauls, the Ligurians were averse to sustained efforts or prolonged campaigns. More than once Roman armies had been saved from annihilation by the withdrawal of the Transalpine Gaesatae, bent on lodging safely at home, or immedi-

[1] Livy, XXIX. 5.

ately enjoying the booty of a first victory. Irresistible in their first onslaughts, the Gauls failed in the long run to reap any permanent fruit from the terror with which they inspired the Romans at first.

As far as we can gather from Livy, the year B.C. 204 also passed without any active hostilities taking place, although we read of the "imperium" of the commanders M. Livius and Spurius Lucretius being prolonged for the purpose of opposing Mago's expected invasion of Gallia Cisalpina. At all events, it was not till the following year, B.C. 203, by which time Mago had crossed the Apennines[1] and penetrated into the territory of the Insubres, that a decisive battle was fought.

M. Livius and Spurius Lucretius had by this time given up their commands to Quinctilius Varus and M. Cornelius, whose united forces consisted of 16,000 Roman and 28,000 allied infantry, with about 3600 cavalry.

We are not told what numbers Mago was able to get together to oppose to the Romans. The battle, however, was most obstinately contested, and the issue doubtful up to the last. It was begun by the infantry, which on both sides held its ground tenaciously, the advantage being rather on the side of the Carthaginians. Observing this, the praetor Quinctilius seized the occasion to hurl the whole of his cavalry on the unbroken ranks of the enemy. Led by his high-spirited son Marcus, the Roman cavalry charged home and were carrying all before them, when Mago opportunely brought up his elephants. Terrified by the trumpeting and smell of the monstrous brutes, the Roman horses, becoming unmanageable, galloped back into the ranks

---

[1] Two passes—those of Pieve de Teco and Santo Bernardo—lead from Albenga across the Apennines into Piedmont. The former pass may also be reached from Oneglia. Both passes lead into the valley of the Tanaro. I reached the summit of the San Bernardo after a delightful three hours' drive from Albenga. The view here given was taken at a point midway between the coast and the top of the pass.

of the infantry, pursued by the Numidians, whose discharges of javelins told with deadly effect on the confused ranks of the Romans.

Having so far borne the chief brunt of the fighting, the 12th Roman legion was now reduced to a skeleton, and would have been swept off the ground, to which it clung more from shame than from strength[1] (as Livy picturesquely expresses it), had not the 13th legion, which had been kept in reserve, come up to the rescue. Upon this Mago, on his side, brought up his reserve, consisting of Gauls. These, however, proved no match for the fresh legion, which promptly changed the aspect of affairs. Warding off the down stroke of the Gallic swords with their spears, and driving back the elephants by discharging their pila into them at close quarters, the gallant 13th promptly cleared the ground of the enemy in front of them.

Now was the time for a fresh cavalry charge, which was brilliantly executed. But the battle was not yet won. As long as Mago was there to direct operations his Carthaginian infantry maintained the advantage it had gained, in spite of the disorder occasioned by the flight of the Gauls and the elephants. When, however, the brave Mago fell at his post before the standard, fainting from loss of blood, his thigh pierced through, there was no one left to rally round, and Carthaginians, Gauls, and Ligurians were mingled in common flight. On the Carthaginian side the killed amounted to 5000; on the Roman to 2300, chiefly belonging to the 12th legion.

When darkness set in the wounded Mago was borne off the field and carried, as rapidly as the nature of his wound admitted of, up the valley of the Tanaro and over the Col de San Bernardo to his ships, which still lay off Albenga. There he found awaiting him Carthaginian envoys, sent to summon him back to Africa, where every

---

[1] Livy, xxx. 18, "pudore magis quam viribus."

soldier was now required to cope with the desperate situation at home.

Having suffered grievously, in his wounded state, from the shaking inseparable from his transport over the mountains, Mago was in no condition to turn a deaf ear to the orders from Carthage. The enemy too was pressing on his heels, and the Ingauni, finding themselves about to be abandoned by the Carthaginians, were naturally disposed to make the best terms they could with the Romans. So Mago, having hurriedly embarked his troops, had himself carried on shipboard, and set sail for Carthage, hoping that the sea-voyage would alleviate the suffering of land carriage. But his wound proved fatal when off the southern point of Sardinia. Thus died Mago, Hannibal's youngest brother and third son of Hamilcar Barca.

Just after his death some of the Carthaginian vessels, getting separated from the main flotilla, were captured by the Roman admiral, who had now a fleet of 40 cruisers under his orders. About the same time, *i.e.* towards the end of the year B.C. 203, also in obedience to the summons of the Carthaginian senate, Hannibal, after sixteen years' struggle with the Romans in Italy, abandoned his impregnable lines on the Lacinian promontory—a sort of Italian Torres Vedras—and set sail for Carthage.

Only four years before Hannibal had received the first intimation of the defeat and death of Hasdrubal by the horrible spectacle of his brother's head hurled into his camp by the Romans. And now, by the death of his younger brother Mago, who had died at sea at no great distance from Hannibal's flotilla, his last hope was shattered. So Hannibal landed in Africa with a heavy heart to meet his crushing and final defeat at Zama at the hands of Scipio Africanus, son of the Publius Cornelius Scipio who had failed to intercept him in the Rhone valley sixteen years before.

By the terms of the treaty of peace concluded with

Carthage at the close of the second Punic War, B.C. 202, the Carthaginians bound themselves to abstain from further intervention in the Cisalpine Province and Liguria. It was therefore with the utmost astonishment that in B.C. 200 the news was brought to Rome of a general insurrection of Gauls and Ligurians at the instigation of another Carthaginian leader named Hamilcar.

This officer, who had been left behind either by Hasdrubal or Mago, observing the weakened state of the Roman garrisons in the Cisalpine Province, in consequence of the outbreak of the Macedonian war, conceived the daring plan of seizing Placentia and Cremona. Throwing himself with a mixed multitude upon Placentia, so suddenly that there was not even time to shut the gates, Hamilcar carried the place by storm and set fire to the city, taking prisoners the 2000 inhabitants who escaped from the flames[1]. In a few hours the great Roman stronghold in the north, which had successfully resisted the attacks of both Hannibal and Hasdrubal, was reduced to a heap of ashes.

Crossing the Po and pressing on to Cremona, some twenty-five miles distant (the two places are now connected by a steam tramway), Hamilcar found the gates shut and the walls manned, the garrison having been warned of his approach in time. Instead of carrying the place by storm as he had hoped, he was reduced to laying siege to it, a tedious operation by no means to the taste of his Gallic and Ligurian followers. This gave breathing time to the Romans, who, by means of extraordinary levies, got together a sufficient force to advance to the relief of Cremona.

A pitched battle, ending in the complete victory of the Romans, was fought under the walls. Their leader Hamilcar being killed, the Gallic and Ligurian host went to pieces, and the Cisalpine Province was once more recovered. The two thousand colonists, taken prisoners by Hamilcar at Placentia, were restored to

[1] Livy, XXXI. 10.

their former homes, and the city sprang up from its ruins. Thus Placentia recovered its position as the great Roman centre in the Cisalpine Province.

After the death of Hamilcar the Gauls and Ligurians of Gallia Cisalpina received no further outside assistance in their resistance to the Romans. We hear no more of their invitations to Transalpine Gaesatae to come over to share in the spoils of Italy, nor of the presence of Carthaginian emissaries amongst them. But the Boii held out for another ten years. At last, in the year B.C. 191, the consul Scipio Nasica, whose father Cnaeus thirty years earlier had inflicted a decisive blow on their allies, the Insubres, achieved the distinction of putting an end to the resistance of the Boii.

Brilliant as was the victory won by Scipio Nasica, it was sullied by the excessive cruelty displayed in the extermination of his valiant opponents. For Scipio was not ashamed to boast that he had left only old men and boys alive. According to Strabo, the entire remainder of the Boii sought fresh and distant homes on the banks of the Danube[1]. In any case, this was the end of the Boii as a fighting power in Italy, and the end of organised Gallic resistance to the Romans in the valley of the Po.

The triumph of Scipio Nasica was the necessary complement of that of his cousin Scipio Africanus over Hannibal and the Carthaginians eleven years earlier. The Romans were now at last completely freed from the supreme danger of a successful coalition between their two most dreaded foes. One half of the territory of the Boii was immediately confiscated, and within a few years the colonies of Bononia, Mutina, and Parma became centres of Roman civilization. It is from the victory of Scipio Nasica, B.C. 191, that we must date the real beginning of Roman administration in Gallia Cisalpina, with which province Liguria was at first officially included.

[1] Strabo, p. 212.

## CHAPTER V.

### THE LIGURIANS.

BEFORE entering upon the subject of the wars waged by the Romans against the Ligurians single-handed, I must draw the special attention of the reader to the claims which this much neglected race can justly make to our notice.

Having been settled for upwards of 3000 years in their present possessions, along the north-western shores of the Mediterranean, the Ligurians can boast of being probably the oldest family and the purest blood in Western Europe.

The late Karl Müllenhof in his authoritative work *Deutsche Altertumskunde*[1], now appearing in a new edition (Berlin), writes of the Ligurians of the Riviera:

"Die Liguren waren hier älter als die Kelten in Gallien und die Ausoner (Latiner, Umbrer, Osker) in Italien.

"Sie gehörten, wie die Raeter in Tirol, und die Iberer an den Pyräneen, zu der vor-arischen Urbevölkerung Europas."

Although absolute certainty cannot be arrived at in the present state of our knowledge as to their origin and affinities, it is now generally accepted that the Ligurians are a branch of the ancient Iberian family, of which the Basques are the only other survivors in Europe.

In his *Nouvelle Géographie Universelle* Elisé Réclus writes of the Ligurians as "probablement frères de nos

[1] Vol. I. p. 86.

## THE LIGURIANS.

Basques;" and the late Emmanuel Celesia of Genoa in his *Antichissimi idiomi degli Liguri* finds many roots common to the Basque in his native Ligurian *patois*.

Some modern writers assert them to be akin to the Celts, and to belong to the Aryan family. But Strabo expressly states that the Ligurians are of a different race from the Celts, although they closely resemble them in their manner of life[1].

The physical type, however, of the Ligurian differed as widely as possible from that of the Celt or Gaul, for the Ligurian was of small stature, nervous and wiry, far more capable of enduring fatigue than the 'Gaul,' whose huge, soft body melted away like wax before the scorching sun of Italy and Provence. In a stand-up fight a Ligurian was considered a match for a Gaul twice his size. At field labour the Ligurian men and women alike were renowned for their endurance.

M. D'Arbois de Jubainville, whose conclusions on the subject of the Ligurians do not always commend themselves to me any more than his eccentric views in limiting the Gauls in Caesar's day to 15,000 combatants, brings them into Europe by the valley of the Danube as predecessors of the Celts. But although I cannot bring myself to accept all M. D'Arbois' conclusions I yield to none in my admiration of the remarkable learning and industry displayed in all his researches.

As an almost necessary corollary of his view that the Ligurians like the Celts came into Europe by the valley of the Danube, M. D'Arbois derives them from an Aryan stock, in direct opposition to the opinion of Müllenhof, of whom notwithstanding he avows himself a disciple. He likewise endeavours to prove that a Ligurian population extended northwards through France and Western Europe right up to the shores of the North Sea, differing entirely from Müllenhof. Nor does M. D'Arbois hesitate to carry his Ligurians across the Channel into the British Isles.

[1] p. 128.

CHAP. V. 47

For Müllenhof in commenting on the passage on which M. D'Arbois seems mainly to rely for taking the Ligurians into the frozen north pronounces it an undoubted interpolation. The passage runs:

> "Si quis dehinc
> Ab insulis Oestrymnicis lembum audeat
> Urgere in undas, axe qua Lycaonis
> Rigescit aethra, cespitem Ligurum subit
> Cassum incolarum."
>
> Festus Avienus, *Ora Maritima*, 129—133.

If, as Müllenhof argues, the insulae Oestrymnicae represent the British Isles, as is generally supposed, a voyage beyond them could only lead to the North Sea and the Baltic[1]. But he dismisses this supposition as ridiculous, asking, "Wer aber hätte hier von Liguren gehört?"

M. D'Arbois is however not any longer alone in locating Ligurians on the North Sea. For in his *La Gaule avant les Gaulois* M. Alexandre Bertrand, also a distinguished member of the French Institut, does not dispute the presence of Ligurians on northern shores, refusing only to accept the theory of their reaching so far north by land. M. Bertrand seems also to rely mainly on the passage of Festus Avienus quoted above.

M. Bertrand argues, that if the Ligurians had spread upwards through Gaul by land they must have left traces of their passage, especially if they were as civilized as M. D'Arbois makes them out to have been. M. Bertrand holds that they arrived by sea, the Ligurians being considered by him to have been essentially sea-rovers, the Normans of antiquity.

Amongst the ancient Greek writers there is a general consensus that at the dawn of European history the Ligurians were found scattered sporadically along the coasts and in the islands of the western basin of the Mediterranean.

Elba is undoubtedly the Ligurian 'Ilva'—a word

[1] *Deutsche Altertumskunde*, Ch. I. p. 96.

repeated in the Ligurian tribe Ilvates located in the Apennines behind Genoa. In Corsica M. D'Arbois cites 20 names of places ending in the distinctively Ligurian termination of -asca. In his work *Les premiers habitants de l'Europe* he cites 257 modern names of places in Northern Italy ending in -asca or a slight variation of that termination of which only 36 are in the modern Italian province of Liguria as restricted to the sea-coast. The reader must remember that the Liguria or Regio IX. of Augustus comprised the entire western half of Cispadana, as far as the Trebia, and that the Libui and Stoeni—tribes of Ligurian stock—were settled also in Transpadana. No similar termination is to be found in the north of France, though not a few occur in the Ligurian district of the basin of the Rhone. So M. D'Arbois' contention is not supported by his own linguistic discoveries.

Philistus of Syracuse, and several other ancient Greek writers, of whose works only fragments have been preserved, testify to the fact that the Ligurians were the original occupants of the seven hills before the foundation of Rome. "Albula," the former name of the Tiber, is, as we read in Virgil[1], certainly of Ligurian origin, as also the name of the town of 'Alba' Longa.

The view that the Ligyes may perhaps be identified with the Libui of the African continent is lucidly stated, although not definitely accepted, by Professor Ettore Pais, of Pisa University, in his recently published *Storia della Sicilia*. The fact that the two most westerly mouths of the Rhone, which formed the boundary of ancient Liguria, were named *Libica*[2] seems to corroborate this view, as well as the mention by Livy[3] of the Libui, a Ligurian tribe settled in eastern Transpadana, near Verona, before the invasion of that region by the Celtic Cenomani.

[1] "fluvium cognomine Thybrim
Diximus, amisit verum vetus Albula nomen."
*Aen.* VIII. 331, 2.
[2] Pliny, *Hist. Nat.* III. 5.   [3] Liv. v. 35.

## CHAP. V.    49

The fact that a fragment of Eratosthenes as quoted by Strabo[1] applies the term Λιγυστικὴ to the entire Iberian peninsula; that such an accurate writer as Thucydides[2] locates Ligyes on the river Sicanos in Iberia, whence they displaced the Iberian Sicani, who emigrated to Sicily; and that a city "Ligustine[3]" is mentioned by Hecataeus, and a "lacus Ligusticus" by Festus Avienus, as existing near the mouth of the river Guadiana in the south-western corner of the Iberian peninsula (known to the ancients as Tartessus, the Tarshish of the Bible), the weight of authority seems to incline to a south-western rather than a north-eastern introduction of Ligurians into Europe.

The foundation of Marseilles ἐν Λιγυστικῇ, B.C. 600, on territory ceded to Phocaean settlers by them is the first historical fact we can connect with the Ligurians of the Riviera. The next is the presence of Ligurians as mercenaries at the battle of Himera in Sicily B.C. 480; an incident in itself sufficient to prove that they were amenable to some kind of military discipline more than three centuries before their conquest by the Romans.

To what extent the Ligurians yielded to civilizing influences in general is much more doubtful. That they ultimately repented of their concession of territory to the Greeks is proved by their persistent acts of hostility and sieges laid to Marseilles and her colonies along the coast, to which I shall refer in more detail further on.

Yet, as the Ligurians had enjoyed friendly intercourse with the Phocaean Greeks while they were building their city and for some time afterwards, it is certain that they must have acquired some degree of civilization by this contact. It can hardly indeed be doubted that the Ligurians of the plains of Provence, represented mainly by the powerful confederation of the Salyes, attained

[1] p. 92.
[2] Thucyd. VI. 2.
[3] Λιγυστίνη, πόλις Λιγύων, τῆς δυτικῆς Ἰβηρίας ἐγγὺς καὶ τῆς Ταρτησσοῦ πλησίον. Hecataeus, *ap. Steph. Byzant.*

earlier to some degree of civilization, than the Ligurians of the Italian Riviera.

Poseidonius of Rhodes, the Stoic philosopher and friend of Cicero, who visited both the sea-board and the interior of Cisalpine and Transalpine Liguria, is the first traveller to throw any light on the habits of the natives. For the history of Polybius, who travelled over partly the same ground when he accompanied Scipio Aemilianus to the siege of Numantia B.C. 134, tells us nothing about the inhabitants of the country. The journal of Poseidonius has unfortunately not been preserved—a loss perhaps even more regrettable than that of the books of Livy dealing with the Roman conquest of Transalpine Liguria. The fragments which remain have been collected into a small volume, in which I failed to find much information that was useful for my purpose.

It is known however that both Strabo and Plutarch largely availed themselves of the first-hand information published by Poseidonius, who appears to have been Plutarch's main authority for his facts about Liguria.

In a passage referring to the Italian Riviera (p. 219) Strabo writes, "There is nothing worth mentioning about it, except that the people dwell in villages, *ploughing* and digging the intractable land, or rather, as Poseidonius expresses it, 'hewing the rocks.'"

Seizing upon the word 'ploughing' in the above passage, M. D'Arbois seems to rely a great deal too much upon it in building up his theory of the superior civilization of the Ligurians whom he adopts as his clients. He cannot control his indignation against Helbig (quoting a passage from p. 38 of the French translation of his work *Die Italiker in der Po-ebene*) for describing his clients as "bien mauvais agriculteurs, incapables du repos, sauvages et pillards, faisant de temps en temps dans la plaine, des deux côtés de l'Apennin, des expéditions militaires, qui n'étaient que de grands brigandages[1]." Yet the above quotation after all closely agrees with the character which both Livy and Strabo give to the Ligurians of the Italian Riviera.

For we find in Strabo (p. 203), "They (*i.e.* the Ligurians) closed all the roads into Iberia along the sea-coast, and carried on a system of pillage by land and by sea."

The truth of the matter seems to be that there were two kinds of Ligurians, highlanders and lowlanders. The highlanders were known to the Romans as *Ligures capillati* (longhaired), and the lowlanders later, as *tonsi* (shorn)—*Coa lunga* and *Coa raza* in Ligurian patois.

The *capillati*, unable to wring even a bare subsistence out of the rocks of the higher ridges of the Maritime Alps and Apennines, amongst which they found refuge, were driven to acts of brigandage and piracy. Like famished wolves, they could only keep themselves alive by cattle-lifting and raids on any food on which they could lay hands in the lowlands.

These *capillati* however clung so desperately to their strongholds in the Maritime Alps behind Monaco and Nice, that even Julius Caesar failed to force a passage through them. The *Ligures capillati* succeeded in maintaining their independence of the Romans till the middle of the reign of Augustus. The monument of La Turbie commemorates their final subjugation, and the opening up of the pass of the Maritime Alps to peaceful traffic by Augustus B.C. 14.

The *Ligures tonsi*, on the other hand, who occupied the lower slopes, and the deltas at the mouth of the torrents which descend into the Mediterranean all along the Italian Riviera, were comparatively civilized even before the period of the Roman conquest. They must in fact have been the victims of the raids of their highland kinsmen before the Roman colonists settled in the plains around Pisa and Bologna. It was probably

[1] Cited vol. ii. p. 80, *Premiers habitants de l'Europe.*

these latter, whom Poseidonius found engaged in ploughing as well as digging.

While the *oppida* belonging to the *Ligures capillati* were mere hill tops surrounded by walls of immense accumulations of uncemented and unwrought stones, it is probable that the towns of the *Ligures tonsi* consisted in part of roofed-in dwellings.

We know from Plutarch's life of Marius, that the Italian Ligurians furnished a contingent of Socii to the army, with which Marius, the uncle of Julius Caesar, annihilated the Ambrones and the Teutones. We find too in the muster-roll of the forces in the opening of Lucan's *Pharsalia* a Ligurian contingent gathered round Caesar himself when about to engage in the civil war with his rival Pompey[1].

It is Mommsen's opinion[2] that as early as the date of the second Punic War, Genoa (the chief trading centre of the Italian Ligurians) stood on much the same footing of friendly relations with Rome as Marseilles. This would explain why it was singled out for attack by Mago, Hannibal's younger brother, who sacked and burned it B.C. 205.

It would also explain the aid given by the Romans towards the rebuilding of the Ligurian capital, which possibly received a Roman garrison. It is singular however that the Romans have left so few traces at Genoa, that no museum of Roman antiquities exists there.

As it was always the policy of the Romans to make friends with some section of the nation which they were about to attack as a whole, it is probable that the Genuates were won over early to play the part in Liguria in which the Aedui figured so conspicuously in Gaul. At the outset of the second Punic War, when Scipio found himself too late to stop Hannibal on the Rhone,

---

[1] "Et nunc, tonse Ligur, quondam per colla decora
Crinibus effusis, toti praelate Comatae." *Lib.* I. 442.

[2] C. I. L. vol. v. p. 885.

he hurried back to Genoa with only a small escort, reckoning on a friendly reception there. For the shortest cut to the valley of the Po, where Scipio expected to encounter Hannibal on his descent from the Alps, lay up the valley of the river Polcevere on the south side of the pass of the Apennines and down the Scrivia on the north. This was the course followed by the Via Postumia leading from Genoa by Libarna to Dertona.

Although Genoa was the chief centre of Ligurian trade, no coins of an earlier date than the Roman conquest have ever been found there. It is probable therefore that Ligurian commerce was confined to exchange of commodities by barter.

Nothing whatever is known of the religious observances of the Ligurians, and no vestiges of religious edifices have ever been discovered in Liguria. There is however a very fine 'Dolmen' near Draguignan in Provence and a solitary 'Menhir' near Brignolles, but both are of unknown origin and date.

It has however been my good fortune to have been, as far as I know, the first Englishman to visit and draw attention to the very striking remains of a series of Ligurian *oppida* still extant in Provence.

Of these by far the most extensive and important is Entremont (*Inter-montes*), hardly known even in France beyond the precincts of the city of Aix-en-Provence.

About 50 years ago the attention of French antiquarians was drawn to the existence of Entremont by the discovery amongst its ruins of some ancient bas-reliefs, pronounced to be pre-Roman and commonly described as Gaulish.

But as Provence was never occupied by Gauls and Entremont remained up to the period of its conquest by the Romans the chief stronghold of the Salluvii, the powerful Ligurian confederation, which occupied almost the whole of Provence, there is every reason to believe that the bas-reliefs in question are Ligurian and not Gaulish.

If my supposition is correct, these bas-reliefs, which are now preserved in the Museum at Aix, are of the highest possible interest, as being the only specimens of Ligurian sculpture hitherto discovered.

That Entremont was an *oppidum* of Ligurians and not Gauls is further proved by the absence of any signs of wooden beams, alternating with layers of stone, characteristic of the Gallic method of construction described and approved of by Caesar (*De Bello Gallico*, Lib. VII. c. 22).

Consisting of two lofty plateaus, separated by a depression from the midst of which rises up an isolated wooden mamelon, Entremont presents a most commanding aspect as approached by the ascent (about 2 miles) from Aix. Both plateaus are surrounded by massive walls of uncemented stones and varying height and thickness. The perimeter of the outside wall which follows the contour of the western plateau, now known as the "Quartier Celony," appears to measure from two to three kilometres, but its irregularity makes it difficult to estimate. The wall is composed of unhewn and uncemented stones of all sizes, the largest measuring about 2 ft. by 15 inches, being laid with some attempt at regularity. The wall in some portions of the *enceinte* is from 9 to 12 ft. high on the outside, but not more than 5 on the inside. The westernmost portion of the encircling wall for a distance of at least 500 or 600 yards presents the remarkable feature of being provided with a raised footway on the inside composed of blocks of stone, raised more than a foot from the ground, as if to enable a sentinel as he paced up and down to keep a look out over the wall without exposing his whole body.

The outside wall, although the most ancient and picturesque in outward appearance, being overgrown with verdure and shaded in places by a fringe of ancient trees, whose roots interlace themselves in the loose stones, is by no means the most massive. The walls, which divide the plateau transversely into separate areas, varying from 4 acres to 6 acres in extent, are in some places at least 20 feet in thickness. Where this is the case they are composed of comparatively small, and generally rather flat, stones.

The area of the eastern plateau, to which the application of the name of Entremont seems to be now confined, is much more limited in extent. The exterior and interior walls are of similar construction and dimensions to those in the Quartier Celony, with the exception of the total absence of the raised footway in the inside of the wall of the *enceinte*.

A great deal of broken red pottery, both ancient and modern, lies about on the surface of the wide wall tops, which serve for refuse heaps when lying near the dwellings of the peasants who cultivate the enclosed areas. There is nothing distinctively Ligurian about these broken pieces of pottery, which have every appearance of being Roman, leading to the supposition that Romans must have occupied Entremont at a later date.

Although unfortunately few details have been handed down to us concerning the lives of the inhabitants of Entremont, yet the broad facts of their history are clear and indisputable, as I shall endeavour to show later on when I bring the Romans into contact with the Salluvii. Inasmuch as Aix-en-Provence lies only 20 miles due north of Marseilles on the Alpine line to Grenoble and can be reached by train within the hour, the plateaus of Entremont can easily be explored in a short day with a return ticket from Marseilles.

Another *oppidum*, hardly less interesting than Entremont, but of a different character and covering much less ground, is to be found on the edge of the battlefield of Aix near the village of Pourrières, about 15 miles to the eastward. It is now known under the name of "Pain de Munition," and crowns the highest point of a long ridge which slopes gently upwards from south to north. The *oppidum* or stronghold is at a height of about 2000 ft. above the sea. As the ground falls abruptly on the north side, there was less need of artificial defences.

But a triple *enceinte* was notwithstanding carried completely round the enclosures, which are all circular, varying from 200 to 500 yards in circumference. The outermost fossa is about twice the depth of the two inner, the bottom of the ditch appearing to be about 40 ft. below the top of the vallum. The exterior vallum, composed as at Entremont of unhewn and uncemented limestones, in its present state of partial collapse is about 30 ft. wide.

As I shall refer to the Pain de Munition again in the description of the battle of Aix, on which occasion it was perhaps utilized by Marius for commissariat purposes, I shall say no more about it here.

Besides Entremont and Pain de Munition, I visited another *oppidum* overlooking the Étang de Berre, marked "Ruines de Constantine" in the map of the French État Majeur, and presenting the singular feature of high, isolated natural rocks being pressed into the service of towers in the line of circumvallation. Les Ruines de Constantine are about 7 miles from the station of St Chamas, following the road which skirts the eastern shore of the Étang de Berre; in a south-easterly direction, about a mile from St Chamas, the road is carried across the little river Touloubre by a perfect gem of a Roman bridge called 'Pont Flavien'—in itself well worth stopping at St Chamas to see. At either end of the bridge is a perfectly preserved ornamental Roman arch—a feature I have never met with elsewhere. The *oppidum* of Constantine, which overlooks the Étang de Berre, is difficult to find, as it lies about a mile back from the main road and is approached by a narrow track, winding through a rocky defile.

# CHAPTER VI.

## Campaigns in Eastern Liguria.

It was in the year B.C. 238, just twenty years before the invasion of Hannibal, that as far as we know the first fighting took place between Romans and Ligurians. It continued intermittently for more than two centuries, the last occurring B.C. 14, when Augustus finally dislodged the Ligures Capillati from their strongholds in the Maritime Alps[1]. No details however of any campaign in Liguria previous to Hannibal's invasion have been handed down to us.

For the first fifty years of this fighting (from B.C. 238—191) the Ligurians were associated with and made common cause with Gauls or Carthaginians, as I have shown above.

After the close of the second Punic War, which was followed by the Roman conquest and the expulsion of the Boii from Gallia Cisalpina, the Ligurians were left to cope with the Romans single-handed.

The next period (from B.C. 191—110) is probably the eighty years' war to which Strabo refers below:

"The Ligurians closed against the Romans all the roads into Iberia along the coast, and carried on a system of pillage both by sea and land. Their strength so increased, that large armies were scarcely able to force a passage, and after a war of eighty years the Romans were hardly able to obtain a breadth of twelve stadia for the purpose of making a public road[2]."

[1] Dion Cassius, 54. 24.   [2] p. 203.

This eighty years' war naturally divides itself into two groups, viz.:

(*a*) The wars waged on both slopes of the Apennines in Cisalpine Liguria, from the borders of Etruria as far as the modern Vintimiglia, in pursuance of purely Roman interests.

(*b*) Those carried on in Transalpine Liguria (the French Riviera) between Nice and Marseilles at the instance of their allies, the Massiliots.

Between these two sections of the ancient Liguria the Maritime Alps interpose, extending in width for about 25 miles from Nice to Vintimiglia. The pass by which the Maritime Alps are crossed is that of La Turbie, about 1500 feet above the sea-level—the lowest in the whole range of the Alps.

It was with the double object of putting a stop to predatory incursions into their newly-settled colonies of Pisae and Bononia (Bologna) and of forcing a thoroughfare along the coast to keep up communications with Spain by land, that the Romans entered upon this succession of wars with the Ligurians after the subjugation of the Cisalpine Gauls.

To the Romans military service in Liguria was not unlike what campaigning was to the English in Ireland in the days of the Tudors and Stuarts, or what it is now in the borderland between India and Afghanistan. Livy describes it as follows: "In Liguria there was everything to put soldiers on their mettle: positions to scale, in themselves difficult enough, without having to oust a foe already in possession; hard marching through defiles lending themselves to constant surprises; an enemy dashing and light-footed, rendering every spot and hour insecure; wearisome and perilous blockadings of fortified strongholds, in a country barren of resources and yielding no plunder worth mentioning, with no camp-followers and no long line of beasts of burden; no hope but in cold steel and individual pluck[1]."

[1] Livy, XXXIX. 1.

Consisting mostly of rocky ravines and forest-clad mountains, Liguria offered so little attraction to the Romans for colonizing purposes that they were in no hurry to annex it.

With the Insubres and Boii the case had been very different, where the Romans from the very beginning were bent on the annexation of temptingly fertile and open territory—territory, too, which if not annexed from the side of Rome would certainly have been occupied by fresh hordes of barbarians from beyond the Alps.

Of the dealings of the Romans with the Ligurians, Plutarch, writing about fifty years later than Strabo, in his life of Aemilius Paulus remarks: "For the Romans did not choose utterly to cut off the people of Liguria, whom they considered as a bulwark against the Gauls, who were always hovering over Italy."

Nor even after its complete conquest, in the days of the Empire, does the Liguria corresponding to the Italian Riviera of our day ever appear to have been a favourite locality with wealthy Romans.

The Romans, being as a nation destitute of the love of scenery for its own sake, did not care to settle on a narrow ledge between the mountains and the sea, where the difficulty of getting supplies must have been almost insuperable in Roman times. While the narrow Liguria from the Magra to the Var was little to the taste of the Romans, the widening plains of Transalpine Liguria—the modern Provence—where the Alps gradually recede from the shore, drew them irresistibly onwards. Here the Romans settled in such numbers that Pliny the elder, referring to the Provincia Narbonensis of his day (second half of first century A.D.), describes it as "Italia verius quam provincia[1]."

It is to the first group of campaigns, i.e. those on the Italian Riviera, that Livy's graphic description of Ligurian warfare mainly applies. For the greater portion of the first series of these wars, or rather punitive expeditions,

[1] Pliny, *Nat. Hist.* III. 4.

Livy is our sole guide. But he is far from turning out as satisfactory in his accounts of the campaigns themselves as his masterly summing up of the style of warfare would have led us to expect.

These accounts are indeed conspicuously wanting in detail, and are sometimes confused and conflicting. For in one page we read of a tribe being almost exterminated, whereas the same tribe turns up again full of fight a little further on. A certain number of names of mountains and rivers are given, but mostly without any indications or descriptions enabling us to identify them. On the side of the Romans we are generally supplied with the names of the commanders, and the numbers of their armies. But in the case of the Ligurians numbers are rarely given, and no names of individuals, not even of the chiefs in any campaign—a most regrettable omission, both from a historical and philological point of view.

However, when Livy's history fails us, as it does after B.C. 167, we only then realize how much we have lost. We are indeed at sea, reduced to a very meagre diet of epitomes of his lost books, fragments of Polybius, Florus, Sallust, Appian, Dion Cassius, and stray rays of light from Strabo, Plutarch, Cicero and others. Orosius, an untrustworthy ecclesiastical writer of the fifth century of our era, whose chief claim to notice is his supposed acquaintance with the lost books of Livy, is rarely of any assistance.

To attempt a complete enumeration of the successive campaigns, for which one has to hunt up and down the last seven extant books of Livy, where notices, sometimes confined to a few lines, turn up in most unexpected places, would only weary the reader to no purpose. It will be sufficient to attempt a brief reference to the more important.

At the outset of the Ligurian wars, Pisae, near the mouth of the Arno, was the base of the Roman military operations to the south of the Apennines, as Placentia was of those carried on to the north. The wide, fertile plain stretching for thirty miles along the shore comprised between the Arno and the Magra, commanded by the precipitous Apennines, had of old been a disputed borderland between the Ligurian and Etruscan nationalities.

The Romans had lately settled the matter by taking possession of the eastern half of it themselves, and dividing it up amongst the Roman colonists of Pisae[1]. Pisae, which had just become a Roman colony, was originally founded by Peloponnesian Greeks from Pisa in Elis. In consequence of the proximity of its harbour to the boundless forests of the Ligurian Apennines, Pisae soon became a great shipbuilding centre and proved invaluable to the Romans in supplying them with a fleet. We have just seen how another Roman colony was established at Bononia (Bologna) to the north of the Apennines on the lands lately taken from the Boii.

Between the two interposed the great bend of the Apennines, where it trends south-eastwards to form the backbone of the Italian peninsula. The intricate valleys and ridges of this portion of the range, including the valley of the river Magra, were now in full possession of the Apuani, by far the most formidable of the Ligurian tribes on the Etruscan border. The Apuani were divided into lowlanders and highlanders, the latter of whom proved themselves such an intolerable nuisance to the Roman settlers in the rich lands below them, both around Pisae and Bononia, by raiding their cattle and destroying their crops, that the cultivation of those territories had to be abandoned.

In the spring of the year B.C. 187, the Apuani, anticipating Roman interference on behalf of the colonists, formed a league with their neighbours the Friniates, who occupied the northern slopes of the Apennines, where they melt insensibly into the plains of the Po. When the news of the coalition of the Friniates and Apuani reached Rome it was considered so grave that

[1] Strabo, p. 222.

both consuls were ordered by the Senate to proceed to Liguria to operate against them.

The consuls for the year (B.C. 187) were Caius Flaminius (son of the Flaminius who fell at the battle of the Lake Trasimene) and Aemilius Lepidus. It was agreed between them that while Flaminius attacked from the north, having Placentia for his base, Aemilius should advance from Pisae on the south. This plan seems to have completely answered. The fighting both north and south of the Apennines began in the plains, from which the Romans easily swept the highland marauders. As the two consular armies advanced, more or less like a double set of beaters at a battue, driving the enemy before them to the mountains, the Ligurians were taken as it were between two fires. Finding themselves caught in a trap in the mountains, to which they were wont to retire, both Friniates and Apuani were eventually surrounded and disarmed.

At the end of the campaign each consular army found itself on the opposite side of the mountains to that from which it had started, that of Flaminius emerging on the south or Pisan side, and that of Aemilius on the side of Bononia.

Of the numbers of the forces engaged on either side, or of the killed and wounded, or of the number of prisoners taken, Livy is on this occasion absolutely silent. We gather, however, from his brief narrative that the campaign was comparatively bloodless, the main object of the Romans having been to disarm, rather than to put the enemy to the sword. The fighting does not appear to have been severe at any stage of the campaign, the enemy having taken to their heels with unusual precipitancy. It seems not unlikely that the lives of the exceptionally large number of Ligurians taken prisoners were spared with the view of utilizing them on road-making. For the year B.C. 187 marks the beginning of military road-construction in Gallia Cisalpina, both consuls, on the conclusion of their campaigns, setting themselves energetically to this undertaking.  The Via Flaminia, the great North Road, the work of the elder Flaminius, which left Rome by the Porta Flaminia, crossing the Tiber by the Milvian bridge, had hitherto stopped at Ariminum (Rimini) on the Adriatic.  It was now carried in a straight stretch of 175 miles on to Placentia, unfortunately not by his son, the consul Flaminius the younger, but by his colleague Aemilius Lepidus, after whom the road has been called ever since 'Via Aemilia Lepidi,' and the country it traverses the 'Emilian' province.

Had the younger Flaminius appropriately carried onwards the road, constructed as far as Ariminum by his father (B.C. 220, just before the second Punic War), and given the family name to it, we should have found an unbroken length of 400 miles of Via Flaminia, extending from Rome to Placentia.  Considerable confusion of names would have been thereby avoided.  For as the reader will find later on, there was also another Aemilius, viz. Aemilius Scaurus, after whom the coast section Via Aemilia was named later on.  But, as it unfortunately happened, the more difficult task of carrying a road across the Apennines from Bononia to Arretium now fell to the lot of the younger Flaminius.

Livy, who informs us that the campaigns in Liguria were full of surprises to the actors, has ingeniously contrived to impart this character to his history of them. For the curtain of the year B.C. 187 having fallen on the peaceful occupation of road-making on both sides of the Apennines, the Ligurians having been rigorously disarmed, we are astonished to find it rise on a great disaster to the Roman armies under the consul L. Marcius at the hands of these same Apuani!  According to Livy, it was the turn of the Romans to be caught in a trap.  Having been drawn onward into a deep recess of a forest, the Romans were suddenly attacked and thrown into confusion, losing 4000 men, three Roman and several standards of their allies, besides an immense quantity of arms thrown away by the fugitives. So complete was the panic of the Romans and their Latin allies that Livy adds, "the Ligurians tired sooner of pursuit than the Romans of running away."

As the Roman armies at this period, and till the radical change effected by Marius, seventy years later, consisted mostly of raw levies enlisted for service in the summer months, like our Militia, it is not surprising that such disasters as that related above were of not unfrequent occurrence. The wonder rather is that the Romans won any victories before B.C. 104, when Marius by two years' drilling made real soldiers of the first standing army Rome ever possessed.

This unlooked-for disaster, which overtook the army of Marcius, was signally avenged in the following year (B.C. 185) by the consul Sempronius, marching from Pisae. Sempronius began by sweeping the Ligurians from the plains, between the Arno and the Magra. This was comparatively easy work, but to dislodge the fugitives from the mountains was a task of the utmost difficulty, as will be readily realized by travellers familiar with the aspect of the range behind Carrara, where the almost precipitous flanks of the mountain ridges are flecked with alternate streaks of snow and marble.

The good beating they got at the hands of Sempronius seems to have kept the Apuani fairly quiet for the next five years. But after this interval the highlanders reverted to their old practice of raiding the Roman colonists in the plains below. It was therefore decided in the year B.C. 180 by a decree of the Senate to remove the troublesome mountaineers bodily and transport them with all their belongings to the Taurasian plains—territory in southern Italy taken originally from the Samnites and still untenanted. This operation was successfully and bloodlessly effected by the consuls M. Baebius and P. Cornelius, who transported 40,000 of the highland Apuani, with their wives and families, to their new settlements in the south[1]. Funds were provided at the public expense to enable them to start in farming, to which they seem to have taken very kindly. It has lately been suggested that a similar experiment might be advantageously tried in dealing with the Afridis. Subsequently, these transported Apuani were known even as late as the reign of the Emperor Trajan by the name of "Ligures Corneliani et Bibiani."

Having proved themselves less obnoxious to their Roman neighbours, and having probably been forced into the war by their highland kinsmen, the lowland Apuani were left undisturbed by the Romans for another year. But as their territory was required for the Roman settlers of the new colony of Luna, which the Romans saw the necessity of planting near the south of the Magra to secure quiet possession of the adjoining unrivalled harbour of Spezia, the lowland Apuani were also compelled to migrate to Samnite territory.

The year B.C. 177 is notable for the foundation of the Roman colony of Luna, on the site of the former Etruscan settlement. This marks the first stage of the advance of the Romans along the Ligurian coast. For Pisae lies just outside the borders of Liguria. Two thousand Roman citizens, conducted by the triumvirs P. Aelius, M. Aemilius Lepidus, and Cn. Sicinius, formed the first settlement. It is expressly stated by Livy[2] that although the territory divided up amongst the colonists was taken directly from the Ligurians, it had previously belonged to the Etruscans.

This proves the accuracy of Macaulay, who refers to Luna as an Etruscan city in his *Lays of Ancient Rome*:

> "And in the vats of Luna,
> This year, the must shall foam
> Round the white feet of laughing girls
> Whose sires have marched to Rome."

There are, however, at the present day no signs whatever

---

[1] Livy, XL. 38.   [2] Livy, XLI. 13.

of its Etruscan origin to be found at Luna in the shape of massive walls, gateways or sepulchres, such as abound in Etruria proper, and have been so admirably described in Dennis's *Etruria*. As such monuments are practically indestructible, Luna can never have been of sufficient importance to rank as one of the twelve cities of the Etruscan League. In fact Strabo observes of Luna "The city indeed is not big, but the harbour is of the biggest and fairest, embracing within itself several and all deep-water havens, and offering just such a naval base as is required by a nation, which has ruled the waves so long[1]." To find the true ring of the Rule Britannia sentiment proceeding from an Asiatic Greek, like Strabo, proves how genuine and widespread was the patriotism of the subjects of Rome. In its position relative to the Ligurian wars, Luna may be compared to Peshawur as an advanced post and base of frontier operations against border tribes. But for the harbour to which it gives its name, and for its strategic importance the colony of Luna would never have been known to fame. For, situated on a fertile but malarious plain near the mouth of the Magra, Luna must always have been an unhealthy and unattractive residence, in spite of its Carrara marble buildings and gleaming white walls, alluded to by Rutilius, the Gallic fourth century poet, as

"Candentia moenia Lunae."

Within 150 years of its first settlement by Romans, its population had so dwindled down, that in the time of the second Triumvirate it was found necessary to plant a second Roman colony at Luna. A century later it seems to have been altogether abandoned, for, writing in the reign of Nero, the poet Lucan refers to it in his *Pharsalia* as

"desertae moenia Lunae."

---

[1] Ὁρμητήριον θαλαττοκρατησάντων ἀνθρώπων, τοσαύτης μὲν θαλάσσης τοσοῦτον δὲ χρόνον. Strabo, p. 222.

How Luna came to give its name to the harbour of Spezia, from which it is several miles distant, and from which it is separated not only by the river Magra but by the range of hills which form its eastern boundary, will always remain a geographical puzzle. That the harbour of Spezia, under the name of 'Portus Lunae,' was used by the Romans before the foundation of their colony is proved by the fact that M. Porcius Cato made it a rendezvous of the fleet that was to sail with him to Spain B.C. 195. It is supposed to have been on the occasion of preparing to embark on this expedition that Ennius wrote:

> "Est operae pretium cives cognoscere Portum Lunae."

In Smith's *Dictionary of Classical Geography*, article 'Luna,' whence it has been copied into the guide books, it is stated that "vestiges of an amphitheatre" are to be seen there. As a matter of fact, as I ascertained by personal inspection in December 1895, there is an almost complete oval still extant, of which the longer axis measures about 80 metres and the shorter about 30. The outer wall is from 15 to 20 feet high, with an unroofed corridor running all the way round between the outer and inner wall. The walls are composed of stones of all sizes, very irregularly set in cement.

Strange to say, there is very little white marble embedded in the walls of the amphitheatre, which probably dates from the second foundation of Luna as a Roman colony. Besides the amphitheatre there are several other considerable fragments of ruins of a nondescript character. There is, however, no trace of boundary walls, ancient or modern. The Luna of to-day is not even a village, consisting as it does merely of a farm-house and buildings, with a ruined chapel attached, a white marble threshing-floor, and several isolated labourers' dwellings. Into the walls of the latter are let medallions of Madonnas, beautifully carved in white marble. Luni lies on low ground about a mile and a half to the west of the railway 'halt' Luni, on the Spezia-Pisa line, and is approachable by a winding English-looking country lane.

## CHAPTER VII.

### CONQUEST OF THE INGAUNI AT ALBIUM INGAUNORUM (ALBENGA).

THE Apuani having been finally disposed of by wholesale deportation, the coast was cleared for the advance of the Romans beyond the Magra towards Genoa. This stretch of coast-line is called by the modern Italians 'Riviera di Levante' ('rising sun') to distinguish it from that to the west of Genoa known as 'Riviera di Ponente' ('setting sun'). So precipitous, however, are the cliffs, especially as far as Sestri-Levante, about half-way between Spezia and Genoa, that the coast is practically only approachable from the sea, even to this day. At the period with which we are dealing, it could only have been occupied by isolated clusters of rude dwellings, settled on ledges in the black rock, wherever a few yards of beach could be found below between two sheltering promontories from which to push off a fishing boat. But even fish are scarce along this inhospitable coast.

Inland, the region is mostly as wild as the coast, the wooded slopes of the Apennines extending right down to the shore. Cultivation is rare, even at the present day, and almost confined to the mouths of the occasional valleys which break the continuity of the mountains. There is therefore little to tempt the few inhabitants inland, or to encourage road-making. Even the modern high road from Genoa to Spezia abandoned in despair the attempt to follow the coast beyond Sestri-Levante, where it turns inland. The old Roman road—Via Aemilia Scauri—may with difficulty be traced a few miles further along the edge of the cliffs as far as Moneglia (ad Monilia), beyond which point it ceased to follow the shore.

The railway, however, keeps on close to the sea, being mostly tunnelled through the black rock, with occasional light and air-holes. This portion of Corniche road travelling has been wittily compared to a journey down a flute.

Considering the nature of the ground, it is hardly surprising that this impossible tract of some sixty miles of coast-line is practically ignored by Livy. We are not even told how far eastward the territory of the Genuatae extended, nor furnished with the name of any Ligurian tribe intervening between them and the Apuani.

To the westward of the Genuatae, the tribe of the Sabatii occupied the coast as far as Vada Sabata—the modern Vado—a suburb of Savona. From the absence of any record of their taking up arms against them, we may assume that the Romans had made an alliance with the Sabatii, before proceeding further westward to the Ingauni.

We have now to deal with the important expedition of the consul L. Aemilius Paulus—famous later on as the conqueror of Macedonia—which resulted in the final subjection of the Ingauni. For the main features of this campaign we are happily not solely dependent on Livy, for Plutarch, in his life of Aemilius Paulus, supplies some material.

As Aemilius Paulus is one of the greatest characters in Roman history, and a very typical Roman, I may be excused for digressing from my narrative to give a brief extract from Plutarch's life of him, to shew what a light view the Romans took of the marriage tie.

"His first wife was Papiria, the daughter of Papirius Maso, a man of consular dignity. After he had lived with her a long time in wedlock he divorced her, though she had brought him very fine children; for she was mother to the illustrious Scipio and to Fabius Maximus. History does not acquaint us with the reason of this separation; but with respect to divorces in general, the account which another Roman, who put away his wife, gave of his own case, seems to be applicable to Aemilius Paulus.

"When his friends remonstrated and asked him, 'Was she not chaste? was she not fair? was she not fruitful?' he held out his shoe and said, 'Is it not handsome? is it not new? yet none knows where it pinches him but he that wears it.......'

"Aemilius, thus separated from Papiria, married a second wife, by whom he had also two sons. These he brought up in his own house, the sons of Papiria being adopted into the greatest and most noble families in Rome, the elder by Fabius Maximus, who was five times consul, and the younger by his cousin-german the son of Scipio Africanus, who gave him the name of Scipio[1]."

I may be permitted to add that it was the melancholy fate of Aemilius Paulus to lose both his sons by his second wife at an early age. For the one died five days before, and the other three days after, the splendid triumph by which he celebrated his Macedonian victories. So after all he left no legal son to succeed him.

The reader will recollect that, after their abandonment by Mago twenty years previously, the Ingauni were left to make the best terms they could with the Romans, in a treaty concluded with the consul P. Aelius, B.C. 201. For the next sixteen years, from B.C. 201—185, the terms of this treaty seem to have been faithfully observed. But in the latter year the Ingauni again rose in arms against the Romans.

The consuls for the year B.C. 185 were Appius Claudius and M. Sempronius. While the latter, as

[1] Afterwards famous as Scipio Africanus Aemilianus, the hero of the third Punic War, the destroyer of Carthage, and friend of Polybius.

related in the preceding chapter, was engaged in chastising the Apuani, it fell to the lot of Appius Claudius to deal with the Ingauni on the western Riviera. We read in Livy[1] that Claudius on the western Riviera fully equalled the success of his colleague Sempronius on the Magra. For he captured six of the *oppida* or strongholds of the enemy, took many thousands prisoners, and had forty-three of the ringleaders of the revolt publicly executed. If the remains of a fortress on the heights overhanging Vintimiglia, bearing the name of 'Castel d'Appio,' are correctly supposed to commemorate the victories of Appius Claudius, they are an indication of the co-operation of the Intemelii with the Ingauni in their resistance to the Romans.

In spite of this sharp punishment, in the year B.C. 181—only four years later—the Ingauni determined to make one more desperate effort to free themselves from the yoke of the Romans. Patching up their feud with their former opponents the Epanterii Montani, they persuaded them to join in a general rising.

If Plutarch is to be trusted, the forces of the combined Ligurians amounted to 40,000 fighting men, opposed to the force of 8000 brought against them by the Romans. This number probably represents a consular army of two Roman legions, without the usual contingent of Socii. These were desperate odds, as the Ingauni, having fought side by side with the Carthaginians, and been subjected to some sort of military discipline, were far more formidable opponents than the more uncivilized Ligurian tribes.

On the present occasion, as soon as Aemilius Paulus pitched his camp in their territory, the Ingauni, pretending to be anxious to make peace, applied for an armistice of ten days, nominally to give time to the chiefs to reason their tribesmen into laying down their arms. The armistice being granted, the crafty Ingauni extracted in addition a promise from the Roman com-

[1] XXXIX. 32.

mander that he would abstain from foraging beyond the limits of the plain on which they were encamped.

Meanwhile, effectually screened by the mountains, which at a distance of seven or eight miles form the arc of the semi-circular plain of which the sea is the chord, the Ingauni and Epanterii were engaged in treacherously massing their forces. All of a sudden, pouring across the mountains, they made a rush at the Roman camp, and were within a little of carrying it by storm.

During the whole day, dense masses of Ligurians surged round the camp, hemming the Romans in so effectually as to prevent any possibility of a sortie. But as the enemy withdrew at nightfall, in accordance with the custom prevalent with Gauls and Ligurians, Aemilius seized the opportunity of despatching horsemen to Baebius, the proconsul at Pisae, with an urgent appeal for reinforcements.

As ill luck would have it, Baebius could render no assistance, his legions having just sailed for Sardinia, nor could any help be got from Placentia, which had been denuded of troops required for a war which had just broken out in Histria, arising out of opposition to the foundation of a Roman colony at Aquileia.

When the news of Aemilius' desperate position reached Rome, the Senate ordered the immediate enrolment of every available man under fifty, directing the consuls to assume the paludamentum (or military cloak worn in war-time in the place of the toga) and proceed forthwith to Pisae. At the same time, the naval force lying in the Gulf of Lyons under C. Matienus, one of the naval duumvirs, received orders to proceed at once to Albenga.

But all these preparations could be of no immediate avail in relieving the beleaguered camp, within which Aemilius strictly confined his troops during the anxious period of awaiting reinforcements. At length, however, despairing of outside succour, the Roman commander ordered preparations to be made for a simultaneous sortie, from all four gates of the camp, on the first favourable opportunity.

It was to the invariable rule followed by the Romans of entrenching their armies within the shelter of a camp even when they halted, *for a single night*, that Napoleon mainly attributed their military successes. On this subject, writing at St Helena, Napoleon remarks: "Pendant dix ou douze siècles de l'histoire Romaine, on ne voit point d'exemple, qu'un de leurs camps ait été forcé. Cicéron, lieutenant de César, surpris dans son quartier d'hiver sur la Sambre, soutint pendant un mois, avec 6 ou 7000 hommes, les attaques réitérées d'une armée de 60,000 Gaulois et donna le temps à César d'arriver à son secours[1]." The experience of Quintus Cicero was an almost exact repetition of what proved true in the case of Aemilius Paulus.

Securely entrenched within their camp, the 8000 troops of Aemilius Paulus could calmly defy the attacks of the 40,000 Ligurians. Day after day, sallying forth at sunrise, the Ligurians approached the Roman camp in order of battle, in the vain hope of tempting the Romans to engage them in the open. At nightfall, however, they always retired to their own encampments[2].

Preserving good order at first, the Ligurians soon got tired of these fruitless parades, and relaxing their discipline, took to indulgence in drink before advancing to the attack.

On one of these occasions, observing the disorder in their ranks, Aemilius Paulus seized his opportunity, giving orders for the sortie for which the troops were anxiously waiting.

The Roman consular camp at this period was square, and constructed to contain two Roman legions and the usual complement of Socii—18,600 men in all. Each side measured 2017 ft.[3] It was surrounded by a ditch

---

[1] *Correspondance de Napoléon I.*, Vol. XXXI. p. 463.
[2] Bina cis montes castra Ligurum erant. Livy, XL. 38.
[3] Smith's *Dict. Greek and Roman Antiquities*, under 'Castra.'

## CHAP. VII.

and rampart, the dimensions of which varied according to circumstances. The camp was divided into three nearly equal segments by two parallel roads called 'Via Principalis' and 'Via Quintana' respectively. A clear space 200 ft. wide was left all round between the vallum and the tents.

There were in all four gates, one in each of the four sides, called respectively:—

1. Porta Praetoria, facing the supposed direction of the enemy.
2. Porta Decumana, furthest from expected danger, at the opposite end of the camp, by which wood, water, etc., were introduced.
3. Porta Principalis dextra ⎫ at either end of the
4.    do.    do.    sinistra ⎭ Via Principalis.

The praetorium of the general was right opposite to the Porta Praetoria. The area of a consular camp in the days of the Republic contained about 87 acres, but Roman camps necessarily must have varied in dimensions according to circumstances. As our military authorities calculate that, in ordinary ground, an unskilled man can excavate one cubic yard per hour, throwing the soil inwards to form the rampart, it would have taken each man two hours to excavate every yard run of ditch two yards deep. As the total 'run' or front of the four sides of the consular camp to be fortified amounted to $2689\tfrac{1}{3}$ yards, it would have required three times that number or 8068 men to dig a ditch three yards wide and two yards deep in two hours. Another hour would have been required for shaping and palisading the vallum. Thus about half the ordinary force would have been occupied on the fortification of the camp, while the other half was available for protecting the workers, if the camp had to be fortified in the presence of the enemy.

Pouring simultaneously out of all the four gates, the Roman legionaries fell with irresistible impetuosity on the half-drunken Ingauni, who finding themselves assaulted from all sides at once were thrown into complete confusion, and offered little resistance. Endeavouring to regain the shelter of their camps, they were pursued and overtaken by the Roman cavalry, who cut them to pieces with great slaughter. It is related by Livy that 15,000 Ligurians were slain and 2500 taken prisoners on this occasion.

On the top of this crushing defeat by land, at the hands of Aemilius Paulus, the Ligurians lost thirty-two of their piratical ships, captured by the Roman admiral C. Matienus at sea.

This double disaster was followed by the unconditional surrender of the Ingauni, who paid the penalty of their treachery and repeated revolts by the forfeiture of their independence. They were in other respects leniently treated, and henceforward furnished contingents of Socii to the Roman armies. Like our plucky allies, the Sikhs and Goorkhas in India, fighters by instinct and with no bond of national coherence, they readily took service under the Romans, and supplied some of the best material to their armies. At the greatest crisis of the fortunes of the later republic, when the Cimbri and Teutones threatened to overrun Italy, the Italian Ligurians in the army of Marius were the first to turn the tide of victory in favour of Rome.

## CHAPTER VIII.

### Conquest of Transalpine Liguria, South of the Durance.

As we hear absolutely nothing of any distinct war between the Romans and the Intemelii we are led to infer that they were involved in the campaign described in the last chapter and reduced to subjection in common with their neighbours the Ingauni[1]. For, *pace* Strabo and the modern geographers, who follow Napoleon in carrying the Alps on eastward, at the back of the Riviera as far as Savona, I venture to think that those mountains should be considered as belonging to the Apennines, there being nothing of an Alpine character about them[2]. I shall at all events take the liberty for the purpose of this sketch of considering Vintimiglia and the Col de Tenda as the Eastern termination of the Maritime Alps. Between Vintimiglia and Nice is interposed the whole breadth of the range terminating in a succession of bold headlands, forming a series of natural harbours just where they are of little advantage to commerce, from the sparseness of the population and the absence of trade with the interior.

[1] Intemelium (the modern Vintimiglia), the point at which the Romans had now arrived, is described by Strabo as a very considerable city, πόλις εὐμεγέθης. It was situated at the foot of the Maritime Alps on the Italian side, while Nice occupies a corresponding position on the French side.

[2] Since the above was in type, I have seen with satisfaction that this view has been adopted in the latest edition of Ball's *Alpine Guide* (p. 2, Introduction).

While the distance in the straight line followed by the railway, tunnelling through the necks of the projecting headlands, is about 25 miles from the Nervia to the Var, the course of the Antonine Maritime Itinerary which follows the windings of the coast more than doubles the distance.

Monaco (Portus Herculis Monoeci) and Villefranche (Olivula) are the two best known of these 'portus' of the Antonine Maritime Itinerary.

At the period with which we are dealing, i.e., the Ligurian 80 years' wars between B.C. 190—110, the armies of the Republic made no attempt to overcome the combined opposition of nature and man at this point. For the ridges of the Maritime Alps, where they approach the sea, were, as I have remarked above, the strongholds of the hardiest and most daring of the Ligurian tribes, who were not dispossessed till the reign of Augustus.

In dividing the Gauls into Cisalpine and Transalpine, as is commonly the custom, we are apt to forget that to make that division exhaustive, we should add the "Gentes Alpinae" or dwellers in the Alps, as they are properly styled by Pliny[1].

The regular armies of the Republic, which conquered Liguria on both sides of the Alps, were almost invariably conveyed by sea, and it was mainly by sea that communications were kept up between Pisae, Genoa and Marseilles. For in Liguria, where the Romans had no intention of settling, and founded no colonies at any time[2], road-making by no means immediately followed conquest as elsewhere. They were in no hurry to provide a coast road convenient for Gallic invasion.

---

[1] *Hist. Nat.* III. 19.

[2] Albium Ingaunorum and Albium Intemelium were Roman Municipia, which differed from Colonies in their manner of originating. While a municipium was a provincial or foreign town admitted from without to Roman citizenship, a colony was a place to which a body of citizens was conducted from Rome.

## CHAP. VIII.

Besides, the Romans had another good reason for pulling up for the present at Vintimiglia.

For Transalpine Liguria, the Λιγυστική of the Greeks, was already occupied by the Massiliots, who had planted colonies along the coast, of which the most conspicuous was Nicaea, in the sunny expanse between the Alps, the Var, and the sea. With their practised eye for trading posts, the Phocaean Massiliots were not slow to pitch on this splendid site, now occupied by the city of Nice, defended on all sides by natural barriers, and wide open to the sea, of which they had just become masters by a victory, 'Νίκη'—over the Carthaginian fleet off Corsica.

Beyond the Var, westward, between the Alps and the sea there is a band of comparatively flat coast, extending some 20 miles as far as the river Siagne, at the foot of the Esterel mountains. This striking range of volcanic peaks composed of red porphyry rocks terminates in the bold headland of Cap Roux, forming the western horn of the Bay of Cannes. From the flat coast half-way between the Alps and the Esterel, a long narrow cape, broadening at its sea end, projects far into the Mediterranean, forming a natural breakwater. On the eastern side of the neck of this cape, the Massiliots founded another city which they called 'Antipolis' (Antibes) or "the city opposite" Nicaea.

It was not till they were summoned to their assistance by the Massiliots that the Romans undertook military operations to the west of the Alps in the region between the Var and the Rhone, which I shall continue to describe as Transalpine Liguria.

It was in the year B.C. 155 that Massiliot envoys arrived in Rome, with earnest entreaties for assistance against their Ligurian assailants. Not only was the mother city closely beleaguered by her persistent foes, the Salyes, but siege was also laid to Nicaea and Antipolis by tribes now heard of for the first time—the Ligurian Oxybii and Deciates. It is somewhat strange that the Vediantii, a tribe of the Ligures Capillati, whose *oppidum*, the modern Cimiez, was in close proximity to Nice, are nowhere mentioned as joining in the attacks on the Greek settlers.

These three tribes, or confederation of tribes, Salyes, Oxybii, Deciates, between them seem to have occupied the whole stretch of the coast from Marseilles to the Var. At all events these are the only names mentioned by Strabo or Polybius. The latter, who was contemporary with these events, is our chief authority for the few facts handed down to us about the beginning of Roman military operations in Transalpine Liguria.

The Ligurians of the coast are not included in the formidable list of Alpine tribes subdued by Augustus, and preserved to us by Pliny, who copied them from the inscription on the monument of La Turbie. They are enumerated, as far as they can be identified, in their order from East to West.

Having given a careful hearing to the representations of the envoys from Marseilles, the Senate decided to send in the first instance three Roman commissioners to endeavour to bring the Ligurians to reason by peaceful remonstrance.

Proceeding to the Ligurian coast by sea, with a small unarmed retinue, the commissioners, of whom the chief was Flaminius, directed their course to the chief *oppidum* of the Oxybii—a place called Aegytna, near the mouth of a river, which Polybius calls the Apron[1]. That Aegytna may be identified with Cannes, and the Apron with the river Siagne seems on the whole most probable. For Aegytna was a few miles to the west of Antipolis (Antibes), and no other place agrees so well as Cannes with the required distance and the existence of a river with flat ground near its mouth to hold the camp which the Consul Opimius pitched on its bank the following year.

[1] Vol. II. Fragments.

## CHAP. VIII.

The competing sites for the honour of identification with Aegytna are Frejus (Forum Julii), Agay, or an almost landlocked bay in the heart of the Esterel, and Encourdoules, a most interesting Ligurian *oppidum* perched on an eminence above Vallauris and commanding a splendid view of the coast, from which the Cap d'Antibes protrudes. In point of archaeological interest, Encourdoules, as I have remarked in the special Chapter devoted to the Ligurians, is worthy of being ranked by the side of Entremont.

We may assume then that it was at Cannes, where the Roman Commissioners put ashore.

But before the whole party had landed, the Oxybians who were on the look-out rushed down from their stronghold and fell upon the servants of the commissioners while in the act of unpacking the baggage.

Hurrying to the assistance of his retinue, two of whom were killed in the fray, Flaminius himself was severely wounded, and barely escaped with his life to the vessel, which lay off the shore. Making for Marseilles, as being the nearest friendly port, though more than 100 miles to the westward, the Roman Commissioners put in there, and leaving their wounded chief to the careful nursing of their faithful allies, hastened back to Rome to report the outrage.

On receipt of this intelligence, the Senate at once sent orders to the Consul Quintus Opimius, who had his head-quarters in Cisalpine Gaul at Placentia, to fit out an expedition to avenge this glaring insult. In connection with this expedition, it is worthy of notice that already in these early days, Placentia rather than Pisae had become the Roman base for operations on the coast of Provence. This fact should be borne in mind in connection with the course of the Via Julia Augusta, the road constructed B.C. 12 by Augustus to connect the Riviera stations of the Maritime Alps with Rome, which was carried inland through Placentia in preference to following the coast.

H.

In this instance too, as previously, in his account of the course of Hannibal's passage, Polybius, although now describing events which happened when he was in his prime, is a most unsatisfactory guide in point of geography. He barely informs us that "Quintus having assembled his forces at the city of the Placentines, marched across the mountains of the Apennines and arrived in the country of the Oxybians[1]."

From this passage the reader unacquainted with the geography of the region would naturally infer that the Apennines were the chief obstacle which Opimius would have encountered in his march from Placentia on the Po to Aegytna on the coast. Not a word is said, directly or indirectly, about the main range of the Maritime Alps, which lay right across his further advance by road. As far as Polybius is concerned we are left absolutely in the dark as to how the expedition really got to Aegytna.

To anyone acquainted with the geography of the district it becomes clear that after crossing the Apennines to Genoa or Vada Sabata Opimius must have proceeded to Aegytna by sea. For, had he accomplished the as yet unattempted task of carrying an army across the Maritime Alps, he must have descended on Nice, and first encountered the Deciates who were laying siege to Nice, instead of the Oxybii at Aegytna, as stated in the text of Polybius.

Sailing up the River 'Apron' (la Siagne) Opimius landed his troops and pitched his camp on the bank near its mouth. After devoting the two or three hours requisite[2] to the never-omitted precaution of fortifying the camp, the Consul, without further delay, led his men to the assault of the enemy's stronghold.

In the absence of the main body of its defenders, still apparently engaged in the siege of Antipolis, the Oxybian stronghold fell an easy prey to the Romans.

---

[1] Polybius, XXXIII. 2.
[2] See preceding Chapter.

As a sharp punishment Aegytna was levelled to the ground and the chief instigators of the outrage on the Commissioners taken prisoners and sent in bonds to Rome.

No sooner did the Oxybii hear of the destruction of Aegytna, than abandoning the siege of Antipolis and without waiting for the arrival of their allies, the Deciates, they hurried homewards to encounter the Romans.

In the fight which ensued, the Oxybii, single handed, proved no match for the Roman legionaries, and were soon put to flight with great slaughter. With the Romans in hot pursuit, the Oxybii fled towards Nice in the utmost confusion, never stopping till they fell in with the Deciates, who had abandoned the blockade of Nice to come to the aid of their allies.

But the Deciates, who had probably been delayed by the difficulty of passing the Var, came up too late to render other assistance than that of opening their ranks to let the fugitives through, and closing them up to stay the pursuit of the Romans. After an obstinate resistance, the Deciates were in their turn overwhelmed, and both tribes were reduced to complete subjection. Neither Oxybii nor Deciates appear to have given any more trouble to the Greek settlers, to whom, as we are informed by Polybius, they were bound to give hostages, at stated intervals, for their good behaviour.

Although the Roman army was quartered in the district for the winter, the Romans on this occasion abstained from annexing any territory, handing over to the Massiliots the strip of coast which had been the scene of their late victories. This concession of the territory was subject to the condition of a right of passage over the road to be constructed by the Massiliots along the coast from Nice to Marseilles.

For the next 30 years, from B.C. 154—125, we hear nothing of Ligurian wars, although the conquest of the Salyes, the predominant tribe or confederation in Transalpine Liguria, still remained to be effected. As this period of Roman history was marked by such important events as the third Punic War, the final destruction of Carthage, and the siege and capture of Numantia in Spain (at which Polybius assisted), the Romans had their hands full of fighting elsewhere. It is therefore probable that even had the Massiliots applied for aid earlier, no Roman troops could have been spared for their protection against the Salyes.

When however in the year B.C. 125 Massiliot envoys arrived at Rome, representing the gravity of the situation at Marseilles from the increasing pressure of the siege, no important military operations elsewhere prevented the Senate from promising immediate assistance. Not only were the Romans free from the necessity of carrying on war elsewhere, but the Senate was glad to be able at one stroke to accommodate its ancient ally, the conservative republic of Marseilles, by sending on foreign service the radical Consul, Fulvius Flaccus, the impetuous coadjutor of the Gracchi, whose land-agitation was now at its height.

Nor is it unlikely that Fulvius started willingly enough for Gaul, and with the approval of his friend Caius Gracchus, in the hope of acquiring by his conquests fertile territory beyond the Alps, wherewith to satisfy the land hunger of the populace at home.

As a matter of fact, the colonization of Narbonne in B.C. 118—the first regular Roman colony settled beyond the Alps—did directly result from the four years' campaign initiated by Fulvius Flaccus. But both he and his friend Caius Gracchus had three years previously lost their lives in one of the city broils, which disgraced Roman politics during that turbulent era. The sporadic settlements of Roman citizens in Spain were not as yet real colonies, and the decree forced through the Senate by the radicals, to establish the Roman colony of Junonia on the site of Carthage, was annulled, when the conservative party in the Senate recovered its authority.

It seems doubtful whether the Romans fully realized

at the outset of the campaign, how formidable a foe they had to encounter in the Salyes, or Salluvii—the Latinised form of their name. Hitherto, on the Riviera, the heavy-armed legionaries had had to do mostly with light-footed Ligurian mountaineers, whom to find was a tougher job than to beat, as one of their historians truly remarked[1].

It was far otherwise with the Salluvii, who occupied the comparatively open country between the Rhone, the Mediterranean, and the Durance. According to Strabo, their territory included the pastures bordering on the Rhone about Arles. This gave them facilities for horse-breeding, denied to the Ligurians whom the Romans had hitherto encountered along the Italian and French Rivieras. Thus the Salluvii were enabled to put into the field a formidable force of cavalry, always a weak arm with the Roman armies before Caesar's conquest of Transalpine Gaul, which furnished an inexhaustible supply during the Civil War, and subsequently during the Empire. Arles itself, as we are told by Ptolemy[2], was a city of the Salyes, being styled " Arelate Salyum."

Occupying a central position at the South-Western corner of the Alps, between the Riviera and the Rhone Valley, the Salluvii are a people who play a most important part in the story of the advance of the Romans into Gaul. Their territory, in fact, forms a sort of pivot on which it turns. Yet their very name is hardly known to British students of Roman history—a fact to be mainly accounted for by the loss of that part of Livy's history, which would have told us a great deal about them.

Our interest in the Salluvii is not confined to the campaigns of Fulvius Flaccus and Sextus Calvinus, but is revived twenty years later in connection with the battle of Aix and the great slaughter of the Ambrones and Teutones in the valley of the Arc. For it was in the territory of the Salluvii that the attempted bar-

[1] Florus, ch. XVIII.
[2] Ptolemy, II. 10, 15.

barian invasion of Italy was finally arrested[1]. All that we learn from Livy about the Salluvii is contained in the Epitome of Lib. LX.: "Fulvius Flaccus primus Transalpinos Ligures domuit bello, missus in auxilium Massiliensibus adversus Salluvios Gallos, qui fines Massiliensium populabantur."

It will be observed that in this extract from the Epitome of Lib. LX. the epitomist in referring to the Salluvii describes them in the first line as "Transalpinos Ligures" and in the second as "Gallos." The term 'Galli' is evidently used here in a geographical and not an ethnological sense. The word 'Gallus' means simply an inhabitant of 'Gallia' irrespective of nationality, just as the name Englishman is sometimes used to include all the dwellers within the limits of Britain. For there is no doubt that Pliny was correct in describing the Salluvii as "Ligurum celeberrimi ultra Alpes[2]." Both Caesar, Livy and Strabo use the word 'Galli' or its equivalent 'Celtae' in a double sense, sometimes general and sometimes particular. It is very necessary to bear this fact constantly in mind in reading the three writers I have named.

Having recently made several journeys through the country of the Salluvii, I may be excused for drawing the reader's special attention to this neglected corner of France.

While the Rhone formed the western limit of their territory, it is difficult to determine exactly where it terminated on the East. For whereas the main direction of the Rhone and of most of the rivers or torrents descending from the Alps and Apennines along both the French and Italian Rivieras is from North to South, in the country of the Salluvii the rivers run rather parallel with than at a right angle to the Mediterranean. The direct flow into the Mediterranean of the rivers fed by the water-bearing limestone of the Basses

---

[1] See map of mouths of the Rhone.
[2] Plin. *Nat. Hist.* III. 7.

Alpes, has been blocked by the interposition of the isolated Volcanic range of the mountains of Les Maures and diverted into a great inland trough, running East and West. About the centre of this trough, dividing it into an Eastern and Western basin, there is a picturesque Col, near the modern town of St Maximin, which is famous for its magnificent church. This Col forms a watershed, dividing the basin of the Arc flowing westward into the Étang de Berre, from that of the Argens flowing eastward into the Bay of Frejus. The Col de St Maximin probably formed the Eastern limit of the territory of the Salluvii, who do not appear to have descended into the basin of the Argens, the lower half of which, including Forum Julii at its mouth, is assigned by Pliny to the Oxybii[1].

Being already in possession of Arles, the Salluvii were now pressing harder than ever on Massilia, which would probably have fallen into their hands but for its remarkable natural defences. For, as I have remarked above, its surrounding zone is sheltered from all attack from the north, whether of nature or man, by an encircling girdle of limestone hills, rising like a wall abruptly from the table-land. Against this outer rocky barrier, the Salluvii had hitherto fretted in vain.

Such then was the country of the Salluvii and such the circumstances under which, in B.C. 125, the consul Fulvius Flaccus was sent to the assistance of the hard-pressed Massiliots. As unfortunately no details of these campaigns have been handed down to us, we have nothing to guide us but the bare outlines supplied by the epitomes of Livy's lost books, the dates of the triumphs of the Roman commanders recorded in the Fasti Capitolini, and a few incidental notices to be found in various classical authors and notably Strabo. We are not even told from what Italian port Fulvius sailed, nor where he landed in Liguria. For it must be assumed that he conveyed his legions by sea to some point on the

[1] Plin. *Nat. Hist.* III. 5.

coast beyond the Maritime Alps, there being no thoroughfare as yet by land.

That this point was Forum Julii, the modern Frejus, can hardly be doubted by anyone sufficiently acquainted with the topography of Provence.

Having reduced the Oxybii to subjection in the campaign of Opimius, the Romans would have had no opposition to fear from that confederation in marching up the lower valley of the Argens.

The striking gap formed by the valley of the Argens between the mountains of the Moors and the spurs of the Basses Alpes could not have failed to attract the notice of the Roman flotilla, as it rounded the bold headland of the Cap Roux, as offering an irresistibly inviting short cut into the heart of the enemy's country. Well might Tacitus, who was associated with Forum Julii as the birthplace of his father-in-law Agricola[1], describe it as 'Claustra maris.' He might have added that it was also 'Claustra Galliae.' Its concave semi-circular Roman gateway—Western Gate—of which I lately excavated the foundations, still bears the name 'Porte des Gaules.'

As if Nature had herself recognised the necessity of a barrier to invasion of Gaul by this open door, she has posted in the gap the rugged mass of Roquebrune, like a giant sentinel mounting guard over the valley. To strike straight at Entremont their stronghold, in the rear of the enemy besieging Marseilles, was obviously the surest way of compelling the Salluvii to withdraw their forces. It seems almost certain that these were the tactics adopted by the Romans.

But whatever course Fulvius Flaccus adopted, a second campaign was required to overcome the stubborn resistance of the Salluvii. For it was reserved for his successor Caius Sextius Calvinus in the following year to

[1] Julia, the mother of Agricola, had also a country residence near Vintimiglia, where she was barbarously murdered (A.D. 69) by the troops of Otho, in revenge for aid afforded to his rival Vitellius.

triumph over them. It is recorded in the Fasti Capitolini for the year B.C. 124, that "Caius Sextius Calvinus triumphavit de Liguribus Vocontiis Salluviisque."

From Strabo (p. 190), however, we gather that the Salyes were far from being completely crushed. This is his summing up of the results of the two campaigns, i.e. of B.C. 125 and 124;

"Sextius, who broke up the confederation of the Salyes, founded, not far from Marseilles, a city (Aquae Sextiae) which was named after him and the hot waters, some of which they say have lost their heat. Here he established a Roman garrison, and drove from the sea coast which leads from Marseilles to Italy the barbarians, whom the Massiliots were not able to keep back entirely. However, all he accomplished by this was to compel the barbarians to keep at a distance of twelve stadia from those parts of the coast which possessed good harbours, and at a distance of eight stadia where it was rugged. The land which they thus abandoned he presented to the Massiliots."

This passage seems to prove that the whole stretch of the coast forming a fringe to the mountains of the Moors and trending southwards to Hyères from the mouth of the Argens, formed part of the territory of the Salyes or Salluvii. The names of tribes other than the Salluvii mentioned by Pliny as belonging to this region must be regarded as subordinate members of the Salluvian confederation.

## CHAPTER IX.

### Campaigns to the North of the Durance.

Although Fulvius Flaccus failed in the year of his Consulship B.C. 125 to earn a triumph over the Salluvii, against whom he was primarily sent, his name is found recorded in the Fasti Capitolini as triumphing over the "Ligurian Vocontii" two years later: viz., B.C. 123. Beyond this bare record we know nothing of this the first campaign undertaken by the Romans north of the Durance, except that, when vanquished, the Vocontii were treated with the same leniency as the Volcae Arecomici and were not made subject to the Governor of the Roman Province like their neighbours, the Allobroges and Salluvii. For it is expressly stated by Strabo that the Vocontii were left in the enjoyment of their own laws[1].

Their territory lay along the spurs of the Alps, including the Mont Ventoux. It was separated from the Rhone by the vast plain of the Cavares, whose capital was Arausio—the modern Orange. Being of Ligurian blood, the Vocontii, with the instinct of their race, clung to the mountainous region at the foot of the Alps, extending from the Durance on the South-East to the Isère on the North, comprising the Upper Valley of the Drôme and the tremendous and inaccessible precipices about its source. The southern capital of the Vocontii was Vasio—the modern Vaison—situate about 18 miles to the East of Orange and commanding a

[1] Strabo, p. 203.

picturesque gorge of the river Uvezes, there spanned by a single-arched Roman bridge. Lucus (Luc) and Dea (Die), both in the valley of the Drôme, were the chief towns in the northern half of the Vocontian territory. All three places are rich in historical associations, and have furnished many interesting specimens of early so-called Gallo-Roman sculpture and inscriptions to French Museums, and especially to that of Avignon[1].

Adopted by Julius Caesar, at the outset of the Gallic war, as the shortest cut from his Cisalpine into his Transalpine province, the valley of the Drôme served as a convenient thoroughfare intermediate between the Valleys of the Durance (Mont Genèvre) and of the Isère (Little St Bernard and Mt Cenis).

When Pompey 20 years earlier crossed the Mont Genèvre or Cottian Alps on his way to put down Sertorius in Spain, he would naturally have followed the Durance valley for its entire length south-westwards, whereas Julius Caesar, having crossed the Alps by the same pass—in order to reach the country of the *Vocontii* from Ocelum[2], would have diverged from the Durance valley near Gap (Vapincum) and struck across the pass of the Mt Gaura into the Drôme valley. This is precisely the course adopted by the little known modern railway line from Briancon in the Durance valley, to Livron in the Rhone valley, cutting the strikingly beautiful Marseilles-Grenoble line at a right angle, at the junction of Aspres-Veynes[3]. As the Vocontii were left to govern themselves internally, being only liable to furnish a contingent of Socii to the armies of Rome, no garrison was left in their country, so that Aquae Sextiae to the South of the Durance still re-

---

[1] Some of the specimens of so-called Gallo-Roman sculpture from Vaison resemble the bas-reliefs of Entremont in their rude features, *i.e.* they may be of Ligurian origin.

[2] Caesar, *de Bello Gallico*, I. 10.

[3] An excellent dinner is provided at the Railway refreshment room and fair accommodation for the night at the Hotel.

mained the most advanced Roman post in Transalpine Liguria, when the war with the Allobroges and Arverni broke out.

For the campaigns against the Salluvii and Vocontii were immediately followed by a war with the Allobroges, brought on by their refusal to give up to the Romans Teutomalius, King of the Salluvii, who had fled to their country for refuge. That Teutomalius a Ligurian should have confided in the loyalty of the Celtic Allobroges, is a proof of the fusion of Ligurians and Celts in a common league of resistance to the Romans. About this time, too, the Allobroges had further incurred the displeasure of the Romans by violating the territory of the Aedui, who even at this early period of Roman intervention in Gaul had been declared the allies and brothers of the Romans. But war with the Allobroges 'the Clients' implied also war with the Arverni, their Patrons, then by far the most powerful of all the Gallic confederations. For, according to Strabo[1], the Arverni, on this the first occasion of their coming into hostile contact with the Romans, put 200,000 fighting men into the field.

But before the Arverni could move this unwieldy force down to the Rhone the Proconsul Domitius Ahenobarbus attacked and defeated the Allobroges singlehanded at Vindalium at the junction of the Sorgue and the Rhone, in the territory of the Cavari. What induced the Allobroges to advance so far south beyond their own frontier, is nowhere satisfactorily explained.

Falling back, after their defeat, to the line of the Isère, the Allobroges, secure from further attack in the angle formed by that river with the Rhone—the island of Polybius—quietly awaited the arrival of their powerful patrons, the Arverni.

The army of the Proconsul Domitius had been in the meanwhile joined by that of the Consul of the year 122, Quintus Fabius Maximus, the Senate having

[1] Strabo, p. 190.

foreseen the necessity of doubling the Roman forces to enable them to cope with the Allobroges and Arverni combined. But the two Roman armies together made such a poor show compared with the masses of Celts opposed to them, that Bituitus, the king of the Arverni, declared they would hardly suffice to make a meal for his pack of war-hounds.

Considering that the battle, which ensued, decided once for all the fate of the Rhone valley, it is surprising how little attention it has received at the hands of students of Roman history. For the victory won on this occasion by Fabius and Domitius at the junction of the Rhone and the Isère was the first decisive blow dealt by the Romans to the confederation of the Arverni, then, as 70 years later at the period of Caesar's Gallic War, the mainspring of Gallic resistance.

Planted in impregnable positions in the mountains of the Auvergne—the central boss of the shield of France—the Arverni alone proved themselves capable of awakening national enthusiasm and of binding temporarily together for a common purpose the incoherent elements of which Gaul was made up.

The aspect of the symmetrical Cupola of the Puy de Dôme rising above an undulating foreground of lower ranges like St Peter's as seen from the Roman Campagna[1] is in itself sufficient to strike the modern traveller with admiration. How much more must the rude Celtic worshipper have been impressed by such imposing surroundings, when the massive temple and colossal statue of the Arverne Mercury still stood erect[2]. The Puy de Dôme was the Delphi of Gaul.

---

[1] As I saw it from the plateau of Gergovia, I was reminded of Mrs Browning's lines:

> "Over the dumb Campagna-sea,
> Out in the offing through mist and rain,
> Saint Peter's Church heaves silently
> Like a mighty ship in pain."

[2] *De Bello Gallico*, VI. 17, "Deum maxime Mercurium colunt."

If Celtic blood is still pure anywhere in France, it must surely be in the mountains of the Auvergne, where the spirit of Vercingetorix seems still to hover over the Puy de Dôme and the plateau of Gergovia. For there alone did the Romans, when led by Julius Caesar in person, meet with defeat at the hands of Gauls[1].

Conspicuous in his gorgeous apparel and golden helmet and drawn along the front of his army in his silver chariot Bituitus, the ancestor of Vercingetorix, and overlord of all Gallia, regarded the Romans as doomed to certain destruction.

According to Orosius[2] the battle was long and obstinate, and only decided late in the day in favour of the Romans, by a panic which set in amongst the Gauls. In his *Bellum Allobrogicum* Epitome XXXVII., Florus attributes the Gallic defeat to the terror inspired by the elephants, remarking that it was "a barbarous method of beating barbarians."

To reach the position selected by their allies the Allobroges in the angle of the Rhone and the Isère, the Arverni had to cross to the left bank of the Rhone. Finding the permanent bridge insufficient, Bituitus hastily constructed a temporary one, by the aid of which his huge army was got safely over.

To fight with a river at your back is, I believe, a violation of one of the most elementary principles of war, for which the Arverni paid dearly on the present occasion. For when the panic ensued, a frantic rush was made for the bridges, resulting in the breakdown of the temporary structure. Many thousands of the Arverni

---

[1] When passing through the country recently, I made the acquaintance of a native 'antiquaire,' who spoke with the utmost contempt of the traitors to the Gallic cause, who sold themselves to the Romans, as if their treachery had happened yesterday. Espasnactus the Arverne, who betrayed and handed over Lucterius, the associate of Drappes, to the Romans, was the object of his special aversion. But I did not observe that in selling a coin stamped with the effigy of a traitor that he asked less for it than for that of a patriot.

[2] *Historiae adversus paganos.*

were drowned, and the greater part of the remainder getting jammed on the permanent bridge or the approaches to it were put to the sword.

Like Napoleon in his flight from Waterloo, Bituitus escaped capture on the field by the sacrifice of his chariot and rich trappings, which fell into the hands of the Romans.

Soon after, however, tempted by an offer of favourable terms, Bituitus was induced to repair to the Camp of Domitius, whose imperium as Proconsul of Provincia was prolonged after the departure of the Consul Fabius for Rome. Treacherously seized as soon as he had set foot within the Praetorium, the Arverne monarch was loaded with chains and sent prisoner to Rome, whither his son Congenatus was compelled to follow shortly after, to share his father's captivity. In the triumph of Fabius Maximus, in which Domitius Ahenobarbus was permitted to share on the strength of his capture of Bituitus, the Arverne monarch, brilliantly arrayed and mounted in his silver chariot, formed the most conspicuous figure in the show. In addition to the honour of a triumph the title of *Allobrogicus* was conferred on Quintus Fabius Maximus, the war in spite of the fact that the Arverni played the chief part in it having been officially styled *Bellum Allobrogicum*.

For the Roman quarrel lay with the Allobroges for harbouring Teutomalius, the fugitive king of the Salluvii, and the Arverni were only incidentally drawn into it. Neither did it as yet suit the purpose of the Senate to annex any of the proper territory of the Arverni. It was sufficient for Roman policy that the Arverni should give up all claim to patronage in the Rhone valley, which was to become the Provincia Romana. Over the territory of the Volcae Arecomici, around Narbonne, which the Romans had long coveted, the Arverni had hitherto thrown the shield of their protection. It was now practically open to Roman occupation, as the Volcae offered no opposition to the Roman project of planting a colony of Roman traders at Narbonne. For at the outset Narbonne was a civil and not a military colony.

The victory of the Romans over the Allobroges and Arverni combined was so crushing that the Arverni are not heard of again in arms, till we read in Caesar's Commentary of their gallant but fruitless struggle under Vercingetorix, three generations later, to maintain Gallic independence.

While Strabo puts the number of the slain at 200,000, Livy's estimate is 120,000. Strabo adds that Fabius Max. Aemilianus erected a white stone trophy and two temples (to Mars and Hercules) at the junction of the rivers to commemorate the victory[1]. His presence being required at Rome, the Consul L. Fabius Maximus withdrew from the Rhone valley, leaving behind him Domitius Ahenobarbus as Proconsul.

The 'Via Domitia'—the first Roman road constructed in Gaul—is undoubtedly to be set down to the credit of the Proconsul Domitius at this period. That at its origin the Via Domitia was designed to put Forum Julii the Roman base and '*porte d'entrée*' into Gaul into direct communication with Narbonne, the future centre of government of Provincia, seems the most reasonable conclusion about the disputed course of that road.

The definite formation of a Roman Province out of a big slice cut off from Gallia Transalpina, was the important outcome of the four years' fighting, which began in the valley of the Argens and ended with the decisive victory over the combined hosts of the Allobroges and the Arverni at the junction of the Isère and the Rhone. As Narbonne which was destined to give its name to the Province and to become the seat of Roman government was not yet ready to receive its Roman colony, Aquae Sextiae seems to have remained for several years longer the residence of the Provincial Governor. But it

---

[1] p. 184. Livy, *Epit.* LXI.

can only have been out of consideration for Marseilles that Arles from its central and commanding position at the apex of the Delta of the Rhone was not at once selected as the Roman capital.

It was a piece of very bad luck for Rome and civilization that the Romans instead of finding themselves isolated at Narbonne at the western extremity of Provincia were not already firmly planted on the Rhone, when a few years later the Rhone valley was exposed to the terrible and disastrous invasion of the Cimbri and Teutones. Had the Romans been settled at Arles B.C. 104—103, when Marius was employing his soldiers on the distasteful work of cutting a new channel for the Rhone, that undertaking, which proved so profitable to the Massiliots, would never have passed out of Roman hands. Nor would it probably have been necessary for Pompey practically to reconquer Provence, when the Provincials associated themselves with the rebellion of Sertorius in Spain, twenty years later.

As a city of the Salyes, who were treated with great severity by the Romans, thousands of them having been sold into slavery by Sextius Calvinus, Arles must have been half emptied of its native Ligurian inhabitants. Lying right across the Roman road into Spain, it is hard to understand why a colony of Roman citizens was not sent there at once to fill up the gap. The only possible explanation seems to be that Arles was considered to lie within the Greek "sphere of influence," to use a modern phrase, and consequently handed over to Marseilles.

The conquest of Provincia being now complete, it became necessary to accommodate it with that first necessity of civilization, a substantially constructed high-road.

Although communications between Rome and Spain were mainly kept up, and military expeditions almost invariably sent, by sea, there had existed some kind of a beaten track, by which the earliest Phoenician and

Greek traders passed between Italy and Spain, along the coast of Gaul, except where they were compelled to turn inland as far up the Rhone as Tarascon—the "Trajectus Rhodani" of the Itineraries—to avoid its 50 mile wide and always impassable Delta. This beaten track is sometimes dignified by the name of "Via Heraclea." The earliest mention of this track is to be found in Polybius, who had probably passed over it on his journey to or from Spain, on the occasion of the siege and capture of Numantia by his friend Scipio Africanus Aemilianus, B.C. 134. Polybius informs us that from Emporiae (the Massiliot trading station on the borders of Spain) the distance to the Passage of the Rhone (Trajectus Rhodani) was 1600 stades or 200 Roman miles, adding that "all these distances have now been carefully measured by the Romans and marked with milestones at every eight stades[1]."

This measured track became subsequently the Via Domitia, undoubtedly the work of the Domitius Ahenobarbus who shared with Q. Fabius Allobrogicus the honours of the conquest of Provincia. But although there is no doubt as to the authorship of the Via Domitia (for Suetonius informs us in his life of Nero, the Emperor, that so proud was our Domitius, one of the ancestors of Nero, of his work, that he paraded over it, riding on an elephant), we are left quite in the dark as to its original starting point.

As Domitius Ahenobarbus completed the conquest of the first province sliced out of Gaul, finishing the work begun only four years before by Fulvius Flaccus, it seems most reasonable to assume that the Via Domitia began at Forum Julii, where the expedition of Flaccus landed at the beginning of the campaign.

There is a reference to the Via Domitia in the oration of Cicero Pro Fonteio, one of the most serious charges brought against his client having been to the effect that, during his proconsulship of Provincia, Fonteius had

[1] Polybius, III. 39.

appropriated to his own use moneys locally raised for the repair of this same Via Domitia.

As no other name but that of Domitius Ahenobarbus is connected by any classical writer with road-making in Provincia, we may confidently follow the authority of Kiepert[1], who gives the name "Domitia" to that section of the subsequent "Via Aurelia" which extends from Forum Julii to Narbonne.

Although the countries of the Vocontii and Allobroges were included in the recent conquest of Provincia, there is a consensus of evidence to shew that the Romans made no serious attempt at this early stage to plant garrisons or make a road north of the Durance, where some writers erroneously locate the Via Domitia.

It is certain that the first object of the Romans at this juncture was to secure a land thoroughfare to Narbonne and Spain. As the direct road from Rome to Narbonne would naturally leave the coast at Forum Julii in order to mount the valley of the Argens to reach Aquae Sextiae by the shortest cut, it seems tolerably certain that the first Roman road—the Via Domitia—originally followed this course.

We must always bear in mind that, as the result of the conquest of the country between the Var and Forum Julii by Opimius, thirty years earlier, a strip of land, varying from a Roman mile to a mile and a half in width, had been handed over to the Massiliots subject to the condition of providing the Romans with a right of way over the road to be constructed by them.

There was then already in existence a Greek or Massiliot road, which was bound to follow the coast all the way from the Var to Marseilles. But this road could only now have been useful to the Romans as far as Forum Julii (Frejus). To follow the coast by St Tropez, Hyères and Toulon to get to Aix-en-Provence would never have suited the Romans, inasmuch as it

[1] Tabula XI. *Atlas Antiquus*. Berlin.

would have nearly doubled the distance and passed through *Greek* territory all the way.

As I have already observed, Aquae Sextiae appears to have remained the seat of Roman government, from which convenient centre Domitius could have directed his road-making operations East and West.

Having dealt so far with the Transalpine sections of the coast road (subsequently styled Via Aurelia by the Antonine Itinerary), the consideration of which comes appropriately after the narrative of the four years' Campaign in Provincia, I will leave the subject of the construction of the Italian or Cisalpine sections till the date of the completion of the road by Augustus, B.C. 12.

## CHAPTER X.

### MARIUS AND THE CIMBRO-TEUTON INVASION.

BEFORE the Romans had fairly got into the saddle of the government of the Province, to which the colony of Narbonne was eventually to give its name, they were disturbed by disquieting rumours of the movement of hordes of northern barbarians from the region of the Baltic towards the Mediterranean.

Beyond the fact, that in the year B.C. 118 the orator Licinius Crassus duly conducted his colony to Narbonne, we know almost nothing of the proceedings of the Romans in Southern Gaul during the twenty years which intervened between the conquest and the barbarian invasion.

We are not even told of how many Roman citizens the first Transalpine colony consisted, nor what resistance Narbonne offered to the waves of barbarism— 'fluctibus barbariae' as Cicero picturesquely expresses it.

Although well-nigh three centuries had elapsed since the sack and burning of Rome by the Gauls, a vague dread of the repetition of a similar catastrophe was still kept alive in Roman breasts.

Yet from the succession of defeats, which the Romans had inflicted first on the Cisalpine, and next on the Transalpine Gauls during the centuries preceding Julius Caesar, it had been abundantly proved that there was no solid ground for further apprehension of purely *Gallic* invasion.

As I have stated above in my Introductory Chapter, the palmy days of the Gauls, when their exploits were signalized by the sack of Rome, Delphi, etc., were over at least two centuries before Julius Caesar. As Caesar himself reminded them, the Gauls of his day had to choose between becoming Roman or being overrun by Germans. For the real source of danger lay beyond the Rhine and the Danube, where the accumulations of half-starved barbarian hordes, pressing on each other's heels, threatened the fertile plains of Gaul, Italy and Spain alike with common invasion.

It soon became clear to the Romans that the invaders, with whom they had to deal in Provincia, were a far more terrible foe than any "Gauls" they had yet encountered. Flushed as they were with their recent victories over the Salluvii, Allobroges and Arverni, the Romans were at first quite unprepared to cope with these gigantic northerners, who had left their homes to conquer or to die.

That the formidable invaders called Cimbri and Teutones who now threatened to overwhelm Italy were of German origin is beyond a doubt. On this point Strabo, Livy, Pliny, Tacitus, are all agreed.

Strabo[1] informs us that in his day the Cimbri still occupied the same part of the coast of Germany, whence they sallied forth in search of southern settlements, and that in his day they sent an embassy to Augustus, to deprecate his resentment for the offences of their ancestors. Velleius Paterculus (an accurate historian who dedicated his work to the Consul M. Vincius A.D. 30), writes of the invaders as "immanis vis Germanarum gentium, quibus nomen Cimbris et Teutonis erat." (Lib. II. 12.)

On their passage southwards, the barbarians dropped a contingent 6,000 strong at the junction of the Meuse and Sambre to guard the heavy baggage, which they could not convey further. Harassed at first by the

---

[1] Strabo, p. 292.

Belgae as intrusive strangers, this German contingent soon won the esteem of their neighbours by their conspicuous bravery and were already incorporated amongst the Belgae under the name of Aduatuci when Caesar entered upon his conquest of Gaul. It is to be noted that in the case of the Aduatuci, half a century had sufficed to convert Germans directly into Belgae and indirectly into 'Galli.'

Writing about seventy years later than Caesar, Strabo tells us that the Belgae were in his day included in the general name of Gauls, and still considered the bravest people in Gaul from having alone withstood the invasion of the Germans, the Cimbri, and the Teutons. We thus find the Cimbro-Teuton Aduatuci becoming Belgae, while the Belgae in their turn are admitted to rank as Gauls. Although there is a line to be drawn originally between Gauls and Germans, it becomes a vanishing one on the Gallic or left bank of the Rhine. For there is much truth in the French proverb, which says, "La Gaule fait des Gaulois."

It was in the Eastern Alps that the Roman legions first came into contact with the advancing wave of barbarism, when the Consul Cnaeus Carbo sustained defeat near Noreia, B.C. 113, at the hands of the Cimbri. However, instead of descending into Italy after this first success, the Cimbric host appears to have made tracks through the central and western Alps, the Helvetian Tigurini being tempted by the prospect of rich spoil to follow in their wake. It was these same Tigurini, as we learn from Julius Caesar[1], who in the year B.C. 107 destroyed the army of Cassius Longinus with which Lucius Piso, Caesar's own relative, was serving as Legatus.

Joined on the Rhone by the Teutones, the united host swept southwards towards the Mediterranean, further swollen by the Ligurian Ambrones from the Durance valley.

[1] *De Bello Gallico*, II. 3.

Between B.C. 113 and B.C. 104 when Marius took the field against them five Roman armies in succession went down before the irresistible northern barbarians. Of these disasters the most famous was the annihilation of the combined consular armies of Caepio and Manlius, near Orange, by the Ambrones—the most valiant of the combined invaders. Their very name according to Plutarch means 'valiant' in Ligurian, and was used as a battle-cry by the Ligurians on both sides in the subsequent campaign of Marius in Provence.

When the news of this culminating catastrophe, where at least 80,000 Roman lives were sacrificed, was brought over the Alps, the sober historian Sallust wrote[1], "quo metu Italia omnis contremuit."

There was but one Roman whose generalship inspired the Roman people with any confidence at this crisis, namely the plebeian Consul Caius Marius, who had just brought the Jugurthine war to a triumphal conclusion. In violation of the provision of the constitution that an interval of ten years must elapse between successive consulships of the same individual, Marius was forthwith elected to a second term of office and Gallia Transalpina assigned as his province.

For almost all the military facts, which have been handed down to us of the campaign against the Cimbri and Teutones, we are indebted to Plutarch's life of C. Marius. As Plutarch had before him the commentaries of Sylla, who played an important part in the campaign, we may rely upon their substantial accuracy.

For Sylla, who had served under Marius in Africa as his Quaestor during his first consulship, accompanied him into Transalpine Gaul first as Legatus to Marius himself, and subsequently to his patrician colleague Catulus in Gallia Cisalpina.

During his service on the Rhone Valley as Legatus to Marius, Sylla distinguished himself by the capture of Copillus, chief or king of the Volcae Tectosages, who

[1] *Bellum Jugurthinum*, c. 114.

## CHAP. X.

was carrying on an intrigue with the barbarian invaders. Of all the lately subdued provincials the Volcae Tectosages alone appear to have openly rebelled. For in the year B.C. 105, they rose and massacred the Roman garrison of their capital Tolosa (Toulouse). It was on the occasion of being sent to punish this revolt that the Roman Consul Caepio got possession of the accumulation of gold which had been stored there and which became so disastrous to his fortunes.

What proportion of his African army followed Marius into Gaul we are unfortunately not informed, but it can hardly be doubted that the services of such trained and seasoned soldiers would have been secured at any price at such a national crisis. Having already paid the heavy price of the sacrifice of five or six untrained and extemporized armies which had proved their utter incapacity to withstand the wave of invasion, the Romans at length awoke to the conviction of the hopelessness of trusting to a citizen army.

It is from this crisis that the institution of a standing army at Rome dates, and that military service became professional.

The African veterans however on the present occasion can in any case only have sufficed to form a more or less substantial nucleus to the newly levied legions, with which Marius started for that ill-omened Rhone valley, which had swallowed up a succession of Roman armies.

That Marius adopted the most expeditious course of conveying his troops to the Massiliot mouth of the Rhone by sea—a passage which it will be remembered was accomplished by Scipio at the time of Hannibal's invasion in five days from Pisae—may be assumed as practically certain. For there was as yet no continuous road along the shore from Italy into Gaul, and, even if there had been one practicable for armies, forty days' marching at fifteen miles a day would hardly have sufficed to accomplish the 600 miles from the Tiber to the Rhone.

Luckily for the fortunes of Rome, Marius was not called upon to encounter the barbarian host till two years after the disembarkation of his army at the mouth of the Rhone. For the Cimbri, instead of making at once for the passages of the Maritime Alps leading into Italy, unexpectedly directed their course towards the Pyrenees and Spain. What became of their associates the Teutones during the Cimbric raid into Spain we have no means of determining exactly. All that is certain is, that they were ready on the return of the Cimbri to turn their attention to a combined invasion of Italy.

The respite of two years, B.C. 104–102, proved of priceless value to Marius. For it enabled him to convert his mostly raw levies, of whom an important section consisted of 'Italian' Ligurian socii, into trained and disciplined troops. For Marius, excellent as he was as a general, was above all first-rate and indefatigable as a drill-sergeant. But although a stern disciplinarian, he won the affections of his men by sharing all their labours and hardships and by his inflexible justice.

The severest labour to which he set them was the cutting a new mouth to the Rhone. Near the village of Fos, conspicuous on its isolated rock on the Eastern edge of the Delta of the Rhone, unmistakeable vestiges still exist of a Roman encampment. These are believed to mark the site of the first camp of Marius, and the name of Fos is considered to be derived from the "Fossa," which Marius cut to give clear access to the Rhone from the sea, the old Massiliot mouth having become choked up.

The second and main camp of Marius, to which that near Fos was subsidiary, was pitched on a level with Tarascon, on the western extremity of the picturesque range of Les Alpines—a mile or two east of the Rhone. This little range, conspicuous for its jagged outline, commands the most ancient passage of the Rhone—the Trajectus Rhodani of the classical Itineraries between

Spain and Italy. It was obviously the best point for military observation.

Entrenched behind the solid ramparts of their camp at Glanum (the site of which is commemorated by a triumphal arch and a perfectly preserved three-storied monument surmounted by statues of Marius and Catulus) the Roman legionaries and socii, now a perfectly disciplined force, quietly waited the arrival of the barbarians.

These last had meanwhile decided to divide their forces for a combined descent upon Italy. While the Ambrones and the Teutones were to follow the coast and cross the maritime Alps by the pass now marked by the monument of La Turbie, the Cimbri and Tigurini were to retrace their steps across Switzerland and descend by the valley of the Adige.

That the so-called barbarians should have conceived and duly proceeded to put into execution this combined plan of campaign, proves them to have possessed no inconsiderable powers of organization. All details however are unfortunately wanting of their method of procedure. We only know that they travelled in huge caravans, conveying their women and children in heavy covered waggons, doubtless drawn by oxen. How they contrived to provision themselves and their cattle, or to cross rivers, swamps and mountains without roads or bridges, we are left entirely without authentic information.

Some faint light is thrown on this invasion of Gaul by the Cimbri and Teutones by the harangue of Critognatus, an Arvernian chief, delivered to the beleaguered garrison during the siege of Alesia[1].

From the speech of Critognatus we learn that on the approach of what we may describe as the German invasion, the Gallic inhabitants took refuge within their *oppida* or hill fortresses with all their belongings,

---

*De Bello Gallico*, VII. 77.

where they were besieged by the barbarians. Critognatus urges his hearers not to shrink from following the example set at the period of the Cimbro-Teuton invasion by their ancestors, in supporting life on the bodies of those who were unfitted to bear arms, rather than surrender.

## CHAPTER XI.

### THE BATTLE OF AQUAE SEXTIAE.

IT was in the spring of the year B.C. 102, that the Marians, from their outpost at Glanum on the range of Les Alpines, at length caught sight of the long expected host of Teutones and Ambrones, making their preparations to cross the Rhone from Beaucaire to Tarascon. As we read in Plutarch, that the subsequent defile of the combined hosts past the camp of Marius at Glanum occupied six days, we may infer that the passage of the river was a very long and complicated business. To the north of Les Alpines there is a wide and fertile plain which extends as far as the Durance, the bed of which is concealed by an intervening range of hills.

In this plain, in full view of the Roman camp at Glanum, were now massed the barbarian hordes, with their vast agglomeration of covered waggons, conveying wives, children and all their worldly effects. For, unlike the Gauls, who at various times had swooped down on Italy and Greece to raid and return home with their spoil, these Ambrones and Teutones had come to stay wherever they could find unoccupied lands.

If, without necessity of fighting for it, lands could have been peaceably assigned to them, anywhere in the south, there these formidable invaders would have been only too thankful to settle down quietly. It was not till a concession of land had been refused to the Cimbri in the territory subject to Rome in Provincia that they attacked and defeated M. Junius Silanus B.C. 109[1].

But so far from having unoccupied fertile land to offer to vagrant northerners, the Romans themselves were suffering from land famine in Italy and felt acutely the need of transmarine or Transalpine colonization on which to plant their own redundant population.

The stake which was now to be fought for was in fact the possession of the soil in Italy. It was the final scene in this early life and death struggle between Rome and barbarism, in which victory had already on five occasions declared for the barbarians. Surely the battle of Aix-Pourrières should have been included amongst the decisive battles of the world. For nothing but Marius and his legions stood between Rome and premature extinction.

In vain, with discordant shouts and insulting gestures did the barbarians day after day advance to the Roman camp in the hopes of drawing Marius out to give them battle. But the purpose of the Roman general was fixed, not to budge an inch from his entrenchments until the first effects of the formidable aspect of the barbarians, whose gigantic stature and ferocious mien could not fail to terrify the Italians, should have worn off. For the glare of the fierce blue eyes of the Teutones, gleaming with newly-awakened appetite for that Roman blood, with which they had so recently slaked their thirst, was calculated to make even the boldest quail. And the presence of the tall barefooted priestesses, clad in long white robes, with the gleaming sacrificial knife suspended from their girdles, ready for Roman throats, lent an additional terror to the barbarian ranks.

And here it is interesting to recall that during the first year of the Gallic war[2], more than forty years after this barbarian invasion, when Julius Caesar seized Besançon preparatory to his first encounter with Ariovistus,

---

[1] Livy, *Epit.* 65.
[2] *De Bello Gallico*, Lib. I. 39.

a panic invaded even the superior officers of his army at the bare idea of facing the terrible aspect of the Germans, in spite of the fact that Marius and his army had given such a good account of them. Possibly in order to serve as some set-off to these Teuton priestesses, Marius carried about with the army in great state a Syrian prophetess, named Martha, who had won the confidence of his wife Julia in predicting the winner at some Roman games, and in whose infallibility he professed implicit belief. When his troops, now accustomed to the aspect and gestures of the enemy, began to reproach their general for still confining them within the camp, Marius would lay the whole blame for the prohibition to sally forth on his Syrian oracle, who would, he assured them, give the signal as soon as the omens were favourable.

Baffled by these tactics and impatient of inaction, perhaps also compelled to move to fresh ground by exhaustion of supplies, the barbarians at last broke up their camp and insultingly enquiring if the Romans whom they were leaving behind them had any messages to send to their wives in Italy, set themselves in motion towards the Alps. As soon as the barbarians had moved off, Marius, breaking up his camp, followed closely upon their heels, ready to seize on the first opportunity of attacking them at a disadvantage.

Marching in an easterly direction, the Teutones leading and the Ambrones bringing up the rear, the barbarians followed the primitive track at the northern base of Les Alpines, which strikes the Durance at Orgon. Orgon was doubtless their first halting place for the night. At Orgon where the river furnished the water supply, which was always the first object in selecting camping ground, there is a cleft in the precipitous cliffs, which there overhang the Durance, leaving only just space for the passage of the old roadway. As the modern traveller crosses the Durance by the tubular railway bridge, which replaces the ferryboat mentioned by Strabo[1] as stationed there to convey travellers over to Cavaillion, he can descry the old track by the river side. But, being bound for Aix, the barbarians had no occasion to cross to the north bank of the Durance, their road only touching the river at the point where it is carried round the base of the cliffs. Two or three days' march from Orgon in a south-easterly direction would have sufficed to bring the barbarians to the hot springs below Entremont, recently converted into the Roman bathing establishment and garrison town of Aquae Sextiae.

That Plutarch should fail to give us any information as to the part played by the Roman garrison which had been stationed at Aquae Sextiae already 20 years, or as to the fate of the Roman population, which had gathered around it, is not a little disappointing. We must however remember that Plutarch did not profess to be writing a history of the campaign, on which he dwells only so far as it concerns his biography of Marius.

Whatever else is uncertain, it is clear from Plutarch's narrative that there were two engagements with the barbarians, and that on both occasions the Romans occupied the higher ground, while the Ambrones and Teutones were encamped in the plain below. For the bed of the Arc, almost dry more than half the year, consists of a narrow and shallow depression in the plain, the banks of which are alternately abrupt or sloping. That both these fights took place somewhere on the slopes of Mt Sainte Victoire between Aix and Pourrières—the Campi putridi—where the final slaughter of the Teutones culminated, may likewise be considered certain.

It was the desperate need of water felt by the Romans which brought on prematurely the first engagement with the Ambrones. "If you want water," said Marius pointing to the river below, in the possession of

[1] p. 184.

the enemy, "you must purchase it with your blood. But first let us fortify the camp." However before the work of fortification was far advanced the thirst of the Romans became uncontrollable and a rush was made for the water, and, what began as a melée between half-armed scullions and scattered parties of the Ambrones surprised at their baths, presently became a regular battle.

For we are expressly told by Plutarch that the Ambrones advanced not in a wild and disorderly manner or with a confused and inarticulate noise, but beating their arms at regular intervals, and all keeping time, they came on crying out "Ambrones, Ambrones."

To join in the battle, which was fought on the right or north bank, the main body of the Ambrones had to cross the Arc. Before they could reform their ranks broken by this operation, they were charged by the Italian Ligurians serving under Marius.

A notable feature about this fight was the identity of battle cry used by Ambrones and Ligurians, the latter echoing back the word Ambrones, or "the Valiant," which Plutarch observes was their own ancient name. This seems to imply some ethnical affinity between Ligurians and Ambrones, but neither Plutarch nor any other writer throws any light on this obscure subject.

Making a good fight of it, as long as they were matched against the Italian Ligurians single handed, the Ambrones were soon overpowered when the Roman legionaries joined in the fray. Driven back with great slaughter across the Arc, the bed of which was soon choked up with dead and dying, the survivors fled in panic to the shelter of their camp.

The reception, however, which the fugitives met with at the hands of their own women was even more terrible than the dangers from which they were flying. For uttering hideous cries and snatching up axes and whatever weapons came in their way, the infuriated women hurled themselves on pursuers and pursued alike, dealing death around them indiscriminately and accusing their husbands of cowardice and treachery.

As far as it went, this preliminary success over the Ambrones was encouraging to Marius. But the great bulk of the enemy was still untouched, and the night following the first battle was a terrible one.

For with the fate of Italy hanging in the balance, Marius had failed in the most ordinary and indispensable precaution of getting his camp duly fortified. And that too when myriads of barbarians were swarming around like bees disturbed in their hive and maddened with rage. For all night long he dreaded a rush in the darkness upon his still unfortified camp, the fury of the barbarians being excited beyond measure, by the slaughter of their confederates.

The Teutones, however, who were encamped at a considerable distance to the eastward, abstained from attack, spending the night and the whole of the following day in making their plans for the momentous battle, which was imminent. As it is certain that the decisive battle in which the Teutones were annihilated took place near Pourrières, at least fifteen miles from Aquae Sextiae, it must be assumed that Marius marched further eastward between the two battles and that he pitched a fresh camp in the direction of Pourrières previous to the final engagement.

The existence of a fortified enclosure on the summit of a neighbouring hill has naturally enough given rise locally to the tradition that the so-called 'Pain de Munition'—the Ligurian *oppidum* mentioned in Chapter V—and about four miles to the north of the village of Pourrières—was the site of the second camp of Marius. But the plan of those fortifications consisting of a triple circle of walls composed of uncemented and unhewn stones in no way meets the requirements of a Roman camp, which was invariably quadrangular, and of vastly larger dimensions. It is also much too far away, and inaccessible amongst a network of intervening hills. It is indeed surprising that a French officer, Captain Dervieu, should have lately published a pamphlet on the Campaign of Marius, in which he deliberately adopts Le Pain de Munition as the second camp of Marius.

Having lately re-visited the battle-field of Pourrières for the express purpose of examining this highly interesting fortification, I entertain no doubt of its having been originally one of the Ligurian *oppida*, which served the inhabitants as a place of refuge in time of danger. It may have been utilized by the Roman general as a place of safety for a part of his stores, but it is a mere coincidence that it happens to be near the battle-field.

Just before nightfall on the eve of the great battle, Marius, observing the very broken nature of the ground shutting in the plain occupied by the Teutones, detached a force of three thousand men under Marcellus with directions to get round the enemy unobserved and hold themselves in readiness to fall on his rear. It is impossible to determine the precise depression of which Marcellus availed himself for his ambuscade, which turned out completely successful.

The fortification of the camp being this time duly completed, the Roman general dismissed the rest of his army early to their much needed repose, which they could now enjoy in comparative security. No alarm seems to have disturbed the quiet of the night.

At earliest dawn Marius drew up his army in front of his camp, probably on one of the natural terraces, which stand out at various levels from the slopes of the Mont Sainte Victoire—the isolated mountain which dwarfs every other eminence in the neighbourhood of Aix.

No battle-ground more advantageous to the Romans could have been selected. For the perpendicular ridges of the mountain, rising like a wall behind him, effectually secured Marius from the risk of being surrounded by the immensely superior numbers of the enemy, and his occupation of the advanced terraces and slopes gave the Romans an invaluable vantage ground over the Teutones drawn up in the plain below. One can hardly doubt that the position had been deliberately selected beforehand by Marius, who had doubtless surveyed the region during his long period of awaiting the barbarians.

While the bare gleaming mass of the Mont Sainte Victoire completely shuts in the north side of the battlefield, the plain is bounded on the south by wooded heights, overtopped by a background of perpendicular rocks, culminating in the Mont Olympus—a mountain not unworthy of its Grecian namesake. No grander setting could be imagined for the trial of a great issue.

The battle began by the descent of the Roman cavalry towards the plain. By this manœuvre, which was completely successful, Marius reckoned on drawing on the barbarians, always impatient of awaiting attack, to a disadvantageous uphill engagement.

Charging uphill, the ground being slippery and the heat excessive, the Teutones, on whom ten years' indulgence in wine and enervating southern luxuries had begun to tell their tale, soon showed signs of exhaustion. They were besides powerless from their insecure footing on lower ground to deliver the cleaving down cuts with their long swords, which the shields of the Romans had in former encounters proved powerless to ward off.

Seeing that the favourable moment had arrived, Marius ordered a general advance all along the line. Up to this point, the infantry, like the British at Waterloo, had maintained its original position on the higher ground, whence it kept up a discharge of pila into the confused ranks of its assailants.

Yielding to the irresistible pressure of the down-hill charge of the heavy-armed legionaries, the dense masses of the barbarians were little by little pushed back down the slopes into the plain.

Rallying, as soon as they found themselves on level ground, the Teutones for some time made a good fight of it. As long as the Romans had the advantage of higher ground, there had been little hand to hand fighting. For while the Romans had chiefly used their shields in bringing their weight to bear, the Teutones had been prevented from dealing effective blows by the nature of the ground.

Now was the real crisis of the battle, the Romans having lost their preponderant advantage of ground.

And now it seemed as if the superior discipline of the Romans could avail nothing against the enormous bulk and overwhelming numbers of the enemy. Nothing but the foresight of Marius in sending Marcellus to fall on the rear of the barbarians could have saved the Romans from disaster at this critical juncture.

In the very nick of time, Marcellus sprang from his skilfully laid ambush, creating the panic, on which the Roman general had not reckoned in vain to decide the day in his favour. The battle which at one moment had threatened to add another disaster to the list of Roman reverses, was now converted into a decided victory. But the bloodiest work had yet to be accomplished in the butchery of at least 100,000 of the demoralized barbarians. At least as many women, many of whom perished by their own hands having previously dashed out the brains of their children, have to be added to the losses of the Teutones on that day.

Never before or since have the plains of Provence witnessed such a terrible slaughter, and rich were the subsequent harvests gathered in, as Plutarch relates, by the Massiliot cultivators of the lands around Pourrières[1]. In addition to the slaughtered, many thousand of the barbarians were taken prisoners to be sold as slaves.

We gather from Caesar[2] that German slaves played a formidable part in the Servile war, B.C. 73—71. But these may have been mainly Cimbri captured at Vercellae the year after. The executioner, who was sent to

---

[1] The name of Pourrières is derived from 'Campi putridi.'
[2] *De Bello Gallico*, I. 40.

slay Marius in prison, when his fortunes had deserted him, is said to have been a Cimber, who shrunk back in dismay from the task.

In the valley of the Arc, the memories of Marius and his battles are still as fresh as if they had occurred but yesterday. Hardly a year passes but what at least one fresh publication issues from the press, and the latest theories about the site of the encampments and engagements are eagerly discussed by the literary circles of Aix.

Nor is it only in the city of Aix, where the battles of Marius and the Teutones are fought over again. If you address a peasant at work in the fields, whose plough has often turned up relics of the battle field, he will probably be ready with some remark referring to the bloody work perpetrated on the field of Pourrières (Campi putridi) 2,000 years ago. The daughter of the landlady of the Hotel Silvy at Pourrières is as well up in her Plutarch, as if she had been a student at Newnham or Girton. Even the village fountain is modelled after the triumphal monument of Marius, the base of which is still extant, close to the high road from Aix to St Maximin. The remains are marked on the government maps as "Ruines de l'arc de Triomphe de Marius."

The peasant, who pointed them out to me as the tomb of a Roman general, informed me that French troops on the march invariably salute these remains of departed Roman greatness.

It lies outside the scope of this work to give any description of the destruction of the Cimbri in the spring of the following year B.C. 101, at Vercellae in Piedmont, where the combined forces of Marius and Catulus completed the work only half accomplished at Aquae Sextiae by Marius single-handed.

## CHAPTER XII.

### THE ROMAN PROVINCE FROM MARIUS TO JULIUS CAESAR.

THE victories of Marius and Catulus over the Teutones and Cimbri had so flooded Italy with German slaves that a servile war was added to the other dangers with which the Romans had to cope at this stormy period.

After Caesar's great victory over Vercingetorix at Alesia[1], a Gallic prisoner was assigned to each of Caesar's soldiers as his share of the booty. As an able-bodied slave was worth about £10 as a labourer or common fighting gladiator, and a much higher figure if he was skilful at any craft, it was in the eyes of the Romans sheer waste of good money to shed more barbarian blood on the battle field than was necessary to secure a victory.

It proved however a highly dangerous game to preserve human beings, like wild beasts, alive for the purpose of sport and satiating the public thirst for displays of bloodshed in the arena. The Servile War, which raged in Sicily some years before the Cimbric invasion of Italy, had opened the eyes of the Romans to some extent to this risk.

But as the victims of the fearful outrages which were enacted in that island belonged mostly to the Greek land-owning class, they were not as yet fully brought home to Roman imaginations.

---

[1] *De Bello Gallico*, VII. c. 89.

But before the Servile War burst upon Italy, the Roman state was torn asunder by a succession of internecine struggles between the optimates led by Sylla and the popular party led by Marius and Cinna, which deluged the city of Rome with blood. The only wonder is that there was any energy left in such a distracted community for the prosecution of the war against Mithridates, or against the Italian allies, who were in arms asserting their claims to Roman citizenship.

That Provincia was neglected or misgoverned, during the years which succeeded the victories of Marius, is in no way surprising.

It is related by Plutarch that in order to test the loyalty of the recently conquered provincials during the period of expecting the return of the Cimbri from Spain, Marius had sent round to the chiefs sealed letters, with instructions not to open them before a certain date. But before the arrival of that date, he sent to recall those letters, which had all been already opened. This convinced the Roman general that the natives were intriguing with barbarians.

The general spirit of disaffection which smouldered amongst the provincials at the period of the Germanic invasion, only breaking out into actual flame in the case of the Volcae Tectosages at Toulouse, was by no means allayed by the annihilation of the barbarians, and the triumph of the Roman arms on the battle field of Pourrières.

To what extent more territory was annexed by the Romans for the purpose of providing farms for the Marian soldiery, we are nowhere precisely told. But we can hardly doubt but that large tracts of land in the Provincia which had been rescued from barbarism and preserved as Roman by their valour, were apportioned out as farms amongst the veterans of Marius.

From that day to this the name of Marius has maintained a firm hold of the popular imagination in Provence. Marius is still by far the most popular Christian name to give to boys, and is strangely associated with the name of "Maria." With the two names Marius and Maria, a third—that of Martha, is commonly associated. As Martha was both the name of the sister of Lazarus, first legendary bishop of Marseilles, and of the Syrian prophetess who was the spiritual adviser of Marius throughout his campaign, there is a wide field open to controversialists in determining the identity of the individuals making up the sacred Trio or so-called "Tre Marie" in different parts of Provence. A very ancient bas-relief carved in the rock at Les Baux near Arles represents three human figures known by that name.

The period of forty years which elapsed between Marius and the appointment of his nephew Julius Caesar to the proconsulship of both hither and further Gaul, was marked by a succession of revolts.

Twelve years after the battle of Aix, the Salluvii, in spite of the bloody scenes which had so recently been enacted in their territory, again took up arms against the Romans. Their revolt, which appears to have been their final effort to shake off the Roman yoke, was put down, as we learn from the epitome of Livy, Lib. 73, by the Roman general C. Caecilius[1].

In the Fasti Capitolini for the year B.C. 81, the name of Valerius Flaccus is recorded as having triumphed over Gauls and Celtiberians—a conjunction of names, which seems to prove that the imperium of the Governor or Proconsul of Gallia Narbonnensis extended at this period over both slopes of the Pyrenees.

We are reminded of this Valerius Flaccus by a reference to him in Caesar's *De Bello Gallico*[2], from which we learn that it was he who conferred the Roman franchise on the father of Caesar's confidential Gallic agent, Caius Valerius Procillus, who was employed by Caesar as interpreter during the negotiations with Ariovistus.

Provincia, the first big slice cut out of Gallia Trans-

---

[1] This name seems to require the addition of 'Metellus.'
[2] *De Bello Gallico*, I. 53.

alpina, the colonization of which by landless Roman citizens had always formed part of the Radical programme at Rome, naturally became a stronghold of the Marian faction.

Situated just outside the political frontier of Italy, and yet resembling it in climate and fertility of soil, Provincia soon bid fair to rival the mother country in the production of wine and oil, which had hitherto been almost the monopoly of the Roman nobility.

Pliny[1] the elder writing of it about two centuries after its conquest by the Romans, describes it as "Agrorum cultu, virorum morumque dignatione, amplitudine opum, nulli provinciarum postferenda, breviter Italia verius quam Provincia." But it was far from having reached this stage of civilization as yet.

To save their lives from the proscriptions of Sylla, which succeeded his triumphal return to Italy from the East B.C. 83, numbers of the Radical faction, which was reduced to its lowest ebb by the deaths of Marius and Cinna, had fled for refuge into Provincia. Most of these, sooner or later, found their way across the Pyrenees into Spain, to take service under Sertorius, who had raised the standard of rebellion in the Iberian Peninsula.

It was the misfortune of Provincia during the ten years, B.C. 82—72, over which the rebellion of Sertorius lasted, to serve as a thoroughfare and to be called upon to support the succession of Roman armies which were used up in the vain effort to put down a movement which was really more like an attempt to set up a rival government of Romans in Spain, than a mere insurrection.

As long as Sylla lived, the Marian faction remained powerless to disturb public order in Italy, confining its energies to sending supplies and recruits to Sertorius.

However, on the death of Sylla B.C. 78, the Marians succeeded in getting their candidate M. Aemilius Lepidus

[1] *Nat. Hist.* III. 5.

elected consul in conjunction with Quintus Lutatius Catulus, the son of the former colleague of Marius in his triumph over the Cimbri. At the expiration of his year of office, Lepidus contrived to get himself appointed proconsul of Provincia.

Had he reached his province, it is morally certain that Lepidus would have eventually carried the legions placed under his orders across the Pyrenees to join the ranks of Sertorius in Spain. But having rashly determined to employ them in a preliminary attempt to stir up civil war afresh in Italy, Lepidus got the beating which he richly deserved, in a battle fought at the Milvian bridge against his Conservative rival Catulus. Upon this Lepidus fled for refuge to the island of Sardinia, where he soon after died[1].

After the death of Lepidus, his legate Perperna crossed from Sardinia into Spain, bringing, according to Plutarch, 53 cohorts and large sums of money to the aid of Sertorius.

In the place of Lepidus, L. Mallius was sent as proconsul into Provincia. But he too appears to have passed very little of his time within the bounds of his Gallic province. For before he had settled down to his work, which must have already fallen heavily into arrear from the failure of Lepidus even to put in an appearance, Mallius was summoned into Spain, to the assistance of Q. Metellus. For the war which Sertorius had stirred up in Spain was assuming such alarming proportions that we find it described by the epitomist of Livy[2] as an "ingens bellum." But instead of contributing to the suppression of the rebellion the expedition of Mallius into Spain had just the opposite effect. For it turned out an utter failure, resulting in disaster and defeat on both sides of the Pyrenees, lending encouragement to rebellion everywhere. Badly beaten in further Spain by

[1] This M. Aemilius Lepidus was the father of Lepidus the Triumvir, of whom we shall read later on.
[2] Livy, *Epit.* 90.

Hirtuleius, the able quaestor of Sertorius, Mallius with the remnant of his legions retreated across the Western Pyrenees into Aquitania, hoping to regain the Roman province unmolested.

But the fierce and as yet unconquered Aquitanians, surprising the dispirited Romans on their march, created a panic amongst them, and put them to flight, with the loss of the whole of their baggage train.

The state of affairs in Spain had now become so critical, that it became clear that Pompey was the only general of sufficient calibre to cope with it. Although still a youth (he was in his 30th year), Pompey already enjoyed a reputation hardly inferior to that of Marius when he was summoned by popular acclamation to save Italy from the Cimbro-Teuton invasion.

From Pompey's famous letter, which was addressed to the Roman Senate from Spain, when he was at the height of his operations against Sertorius, we learn the interesting fact, that at the moment of Pompey's appointment the war had spread over Provincia right up to the Alps.

This daring attempt on the part of Sertorius to carry his forces across the Alps and transfer the field of his operations to Italy appears to have been completely frustrated by Pompey, if we are to believe his own account of it.

As being the first occasion on which a Roman army was ever, as far as we know, carried across the Alps, the passage of Pompey is singularly interesting to us. Hitherto in their successive invasions of Provincia, as we have seen, the Roman legions had been conveyed to their destination by sea.

But now that the forces under Sertorius were reported to be scaling the Alps, it was necessary to send an army by land to oppose their passage. Unfortunately, the letter of Pompey to the Senate only refers incidentally to his passage of the Alps, and his encounter with Sertorius. It runs thus:—" Having equipped my army in the short space of forty days, I pushed the enemy, whom I found threatening Italy from the Alps, right back into Spain, having opened up a new road through the Alps, more convenient for us than that by which Hannibal crossed."

"I won back Provincia as far as the Pyrenees to our allegiance, and successfully bore the brunt of the attack of Sertorius' victorious veterans with my untrained troops[1]."

The new route over the Alps referred to by Pompey as more convenient 'to us' can have been no other than that of the Mont Genèvre. For it must be fixed to the south of Hannibal's road (by the Mt Cenis) in order to make it more convenient for reaching Arles and Spain, for which he was bound.

To anyone sufficiently familiar with the Alps to enable him to make a comparison between the Mont Genèvre and other passes, it can excite no wonder that the Romans adopted it as their favourite line of communication between North Italy and Spain across the Roman Province. For it presents hardly any of the features and difficulties incident to the ordinary Alpine pass.

At the highest point of the so-called Pass, which is about the same elevation as the Rigi-Culm, the road is carried for two or three miles almost on the level, across a broad plateau commanded by heights crowned with pine and larch. In the centre lies the smiling village of Mt Genèvre with its neat church surmounted by a stone spire. It is by a long way the most human of the Alpine passes, and a spot, where you feel disposed to linger rather than to hurry through. If other considerations did not prevent us from adopting it as Hannibal's pass, the sunny plateau would have been most suitable for the two days' rest, which Hannibal is said by Livy to have given to his tired-out followers on the summit. The classical name of the mountain top

[1] Sallust. Appended to the Teubner Edition of the Bellum Jugurthinum.

'Mons Matrona' seems strictly in harmony with the 'genius loci,' offering as it does a broad lap for the repose of the weary.

In the same letter to the Senate, Pompey represents the urgent need in which he stood of money and supplies. He threatens the Senate with the almost certain prospect of the transfer of the war into Italy, owing to the exhaustion of supplies both in Spain and Provincia, adding that owing to a failure of the harvest in the latter country, there was barely enough corn for the inhabitants. This threat conveyed in Pompey's letter seems to have brought the Senate to its senses. For money and supplies were dispatched in response to it, and the insurrection of Sertorius was henceforth confined to Spain.

In what remains to us of his oration on behalf of M. Fonteius, who was governor of the Provincia Romana during three years of the period during which Pompey was operating against Sertorius, *i.e.* from 76 to 74 B.C., Cicero supplies us with some valuable material for forming a picture of the state of Provincia at that period. Entrusted by Pompey with the pacification of the province and with the execution of his decrees of confiscation of the estates of the provincials, who had joined in the rebellion of Sertorius, Fonteius appears to have carried out his commission so rigorously and to have exasperated the natives so effectually, that five years after his retirement they got him brought to trial at Rome on the charge of extortion and embezzlement of public funds.

That the rebellion in Provincia was widespread and formidable is proved by the important fact, which we learn solely from the speech of Cicero, that the insurgents even laid siege to the Roman colony of Narbonne. That Fonteius successfully relieved the capital from falling into their hands is dwelt upon by Cicero as one of his client's titles to the enduring gratitude of the Roman settlers in the earliest colony in Gaul.

In appraising the value of Cicero's estimate of the Gallic element in the population of Provincia, we must always bear in mind that he speaks as an advocate, endeavouring to get a verdict of acquittal from a prejudiced Roman jury.

Had Cicero been retained for the prosecution, we can easily imagine from reading between the lines of his defence, what a case might have been made out against his client Fonteius by the orator, who had denounced Verres so vigorously only the year previously (B.C. 70).

In picturing the Gauls as the enemies of all religion, and referring to their former exploits in besieging Jupiter in his temple at Rome on the Capitoline Hill and outraging the oracle of Apollo at Delphi, Cicero raked up old stories which were as irrelevant as the addresses of advocates in our own time often are.

In going on to accuse the Gauls of the Provincia of his day as continuing the practice of human sacrifice, in order to discredit them as witnesses, it looks as if he must wilfully have departed from the truth. For only 20 years later, Julius Caesar[1] expressly remarks on the superior "cultus atque humanitas" which distinguished Provincia from the rest of Gaul. After this highly coloured and distorted description of the Gauls, Cicero proceeds thus :

"In this same Provincia, there is planted Narbo Martius, a colony of our own citizens—the very image of the Roman people, an advanced post of civilization thrown into the jaws of those savages. There is too the city of Marseilles—a community of our most valiant and trusty allies, who from time immemorial have stood by us in sharing the risks and burdens of Gallic wars. There is, too, an unlimited number of Roman citizens, most trustworthy individuals."

Further on, Cicero remarks " Besides, while Fonteius was governor, the numerous and fully equipped army of Cnaeus Pompeius was quartered for a whole winter in

[1] *De Bello Gallico*, I. 1.

the Roman Province, which was crammed full of Roman knights, military tribunes and legates, constantly passing backwards and forwards between the armies and generals in both the Spanish provinces[1]."

That not a single one of these honourable Romans could be got to bear witness against Fonteius was, according to Cicero, sufficient proof of the innocence of his client.

However, with the guilt or innocence of Fonteius we are not here concerned. It is sufficient for us that Cicero admits and puts it down to his client's credit, that he extracted from the unfortunate provincials immense sums of money and supplies of corn to carry on the war in Spain, in addition to providing the Roman armies all over the globe with complements of cavalry.

We are not specifically informed, which native tribes were the ringleaders in the revolt of the provincials, put down by Pompey's legate Fonteius. But we gather from a reference in the *De Bello Civili*, I. 35 that it was the Volcae and Helvii, who were on this occasion mulcted of territory which Pompey handed over to the Republic of Marseilles, acquiring thereby its support when the Civil War broke out between him and Julius Caesar.

Although the Allobroges are represented as being loudest in their complaints against Fonteius, it is doubtful whether they actually took up arms against his exactions. At all events, their territory lying as it did well out of reach of annexation by the Republic of Marseilles was left to them whole, although subjected to heavy taxation and arbitrary exactions.

Within the next few years, however, they broke out twice into open insurrections, the first of which was put down by Calpurnius Piso in B.C. 66, and the second by C. Pomptinus in 61.

Between these two risings, namely in the year of

[1] *Oratio pro M. Fonteio*, ch. 13—16.

Cicero's consulship B.C. 63, the Allobroges sent an embassy to Rome to endeavour to get some redress from the Senate from the unbearable exactions of the Provincial governors. It so happened that the presence of their ambassadors in Rome coincided with the plotting of the Catiline conspiracy.

Disappointed in their hopes of getting satisfaction from the Senate, the ambassadors of the Allobroges were approached by the leaders of the Catiline conspiracy, who promised them complete redress of their grievances, in the event of their contributing to make the conspiracy successful by getting up a rising in their own country.

Feigning readiness to co-operate in the manner indicated by the conspirators, and having obtained written promises of rewards from the authors of the conspiracy, the ambassadors of the Allobroges left Rome at night-fall on their homeward journey.

They had, however, already betrayed the secret of their negotiations to Cicero, the consul, who by agreement with them had made arrangements to have the whole party arrested at the Milvian bridge, about a mile and a half to the north of the city, where the Via Flaminia crosses the Tiber.

On the indisputable evidence of the compromising documents seized on the persons of the Ambassadors, Lentulus and Cethegus, two of the leading conspirators, were arrested by Cicero, and shortly afterwards summarily put to death. Although Catiline himself contrived to escape from the city and openly raised the standard of rebellion in Etruria, the danger of a rising at Rome was averted. But in spite of this important service rendered to the Republic by their ambassadors at this crisis, the Roman Senate continued to turn a deaf ear to the legitimate complaints of the Allobroges.

Having exhausted every expedient of getting redress by peaceful means, the Allobroges were at last provoked into taking up arms, but not in conjunction with the conspiracy of Catiline. For that rebellion had been effectually stamped out, before Cicero and the Senate dared finally to reject the appeal of the Allobroges for more lenient treatment.

The praetor Caius Pomptinus, who had been Cicero's right hand man in the suppression of the Catiline conspiracy, was now sent into the Roman Province, with the commission to spare no severity in the repression of the rising of the Allobroges.

But before his arrival on the scene, Catugnatus the leader of the Allobroges so completely out-generalled Manlius Lentinus, the legate of Pomptinus, that the Roman army was only saved from destruction by the occurrence of a tempest of unusual violence.

When however Pomptinus took the field in person, he soon turned the tables upon the enemy, and having contrived to draw a cordon around the insurgent forces, made prisoners of the whole. Catugnatus nevertheless contrived to escape.

The rebellion of the Allobroges being thus effectually put down, Pomptinus set out for Rome confidently anticipating that the Senate would grant him the honours of the triumph, to which he considered himself justly entitled. In this expectation he was however doomed to disappointment. For taking advantage of a technical irregularity in the conferring of his 'imperium' his enemies in the Senate were successful in preventing the passing of the requisite decree.

So determined however was Pomptinus to achieve his purpose in spite of the Senate, that he had the patience to wait six whole years outside the city, taking up his residence in the Pomoerium. Had he set foot within the city, his chance of triumphing would have been forfeited.

This extraordinary patience was ultimately rewarded. For although the Senate persisted in its refusal, Servius Sulpicius Galba, who had formerly served as legate under Pomptinus, got a triumph voted by popular resolution, B.C. 54. Although it was alleged that this resolution was illegal, as having been carried before daylight, Pomptinus was notwithstanding permitted to enjoy the honours of a triumph.

That he richly deserved them for the signal services rendered to the Republic can hardly be doubted. For up to their final reduction by Pomptinus B.C. 61, the Allobroges had been a constant source of trouble to the Romans, having been in a chronic state of secret or open rebellion.

Chafing under the Roman yoke from which their more fortunate Ligurian neighbours, the Vocontii, were left entirely free, the Allobroges were keenly sensible of their inferior status as mere provincial subjects of Rome.

The attempt to govern such a restless people from distant centres, such as Aquae Sextiae or Narbonne, having entirely broken down, Vienna (Vienne-en-Dauphiné) now became the seat of Roman administration of the country comprised between the Isère, the Rhone and the Alps.

## CHAPTER XIII.

### THE PROVINCIA ROMANA IN RELATION TO CAESAR'S GALLIC AND CIVIL WARS.

WITH the appearance of Julius Caesar in Gaul and his assumption of the reins of government in Provincia, the relations of the Allobroges to the Romans underwent a radical change. Realizing that the country of the Allobroges was the most convenient, if not the only possible, base for his operations in Gallia Comata—the 'omnis Gallia' of the *De Bello Gallico*—Caesar determined to secure their friendship at any price. As if by magic, from having been the most troublesome people in Transalpine Gaul, the Allobroges suddenly became the most loyal, and remained the most steadfast allies of the Romans throughout the whole period of Caesar's Gallic Wars.

Even when the constancy of the Aedui broke down, in spite of their sworn brotherhood with the Romans, at the critical moment following the repulse of the Romans from Gergovia, the Allobroges remained true. Had they also been induced to join in the national rising and yielded to the solicitation of Vercingetorix, it would in all probability have been all over with the fortunes of Caesar, and the course of Roman history would have been diverted into an entirely different channel.

By what specific means Caesar succeeded in winning over the affections of the Allobroges, we are not, as far as I can discover, directly informed by any classical authority. But from a somewhat rare and much-esteemed local work[1], of which I made an analysis from a copy borrowed during my journey through the country, I have derived much useful information bearing on the subject.

It is stated by Pitot that Pomptinus, the predecessor of Julius Caesar in the governorship of Provincia after his final subjugation of the Allobroges, established at Vienna a colony of Roman and Italian veterans. Although I failed to note his authority for this statement, it is practically certain, that under the rule of Pomptinus Vienna became for the first time the seat of Roman Government in Northern Provincia, which was bounded by the course of the Rhone as far as Geneva.

Already in the days of Hannibal, a century and a half earlier, the existence of a 'senate' of the Allobroges is mentioned by Livy where he states that the decision of the Carthaginian leader in favour of the elder disputant for the chieftainship was agreeable to 'the Senate' and chiefs of the nation.

That this 'Senate' was entirely suppressed during the rigorous regime of Pomptinus seems more than probable. To restore it partially, and remodel it on a safe basis, appears to have been a leading feature in Caesar's new scheme of government. But as out of 100 seats 25 only were assigned to Allobroges, it is difficult to understand how this arrangement can have been accepted even for a time by the native population. The theory that Caesar, like Napoleon, exercised a magnetic influence over the Gallic race, alone explains much that would be otherwise unintelligible in his dealings with the Gauls.

That Caesar took an active part in the formation of the Senate of the Allobroges is proved by the fact that he caused his native associates and particular friends— Raucillus and Egus, sons of Abducillus, for many years chief of the state—to be elected supernumerary members

[1] "Recherches sur les Antiquités Dauphinoises, par J. J. A. Pitot." (Baratier, Grenoble, 1833.)

of that body, having previously endowed them with estates in land confiscated in Gaul (Gallia Comata).

That the temporary loyalty of the Allobroges is to be attributed solely to their devotion to the personality of Julius Caesar seems proved by the fact that no sooner did they hear of his assassination than they rose *en masse* and expelled the entire body of Roman and Italian colonists out of Vienna.

Instead of severely punishing the authors of this outrage, the Roman Senate, in the confusion following the murder of Caesar, contented itself with sending orders to Plancus, governor of Gallia Ulterior—to conduct the colonists expelled from Vienna to found a Roman Colony at Lugdunum.

Such was the origin of Roman Lyons, between which city and Vienna a lasting feud existed.

The importance of Vienna to Caesar in the prosecution of his Gallic Wars can hardly be exaggerated. In Caesar's day it was the last outpost of the comparative civilization of the Roman Province against the outer barbarism of Gallia Comata or Gaul beyond the Rhone. For Lyons (Lugdunum) in spite of its convenient position at the junction of the Saone and the Rhone, was as yet a place of no importance and quite ignored by Julius Caesar, although it was soon to become under Augustus the Roman capital of Gaul.

In order to render Vienna the impregnable frontier fortress which he required, Caesar employed on strengthening its fortifications the bulk of the prisoners taken in his earliest battles in Gaul. Between the years B.C. 58—56, forty thousand labourers are said to have been engaged on this work.

Vienna now received its title of 'Colonia Julia Viennensis,' and became the first 'Caput' of the Roman roads leading over the Alps into Gallia Transalpina.

Planted on a series of picturesque heights and terraces commanding a great bend of the Rhone, Vienna is naturally a place of great strength, and presents a most striking appearance when viewed from the river. From the express trains, which pass by the P. L. M. Station of Vienne-en-Dauphiné (half an hour below Lyons) in a dark cutting or darker tunnel, you see nothing that is striking in the place, as you rush through. Vienne is however well worth stopping at and exploring, both for its Roman and mediaeval antiquities. For after it had lost much of its civil importance to the Romans by the transference of the seat of the government of the whole of Gaul to Lyons, Vienna soon acquired and has retained to this day a Metropolitan character in ecclesiastical jurisdiction.

When in the year B.C. 52, after six years' fighting with almost uninterrupted success, it seemed that the conquest of Gaul had been practically achieved, Vercingetorix succeeded in exciting his countrymen to a final effort to escape from the Roman yoke; he saw at a glance that his best chance was to strike at Provincia and endeavour to cut the Romans off from their base. Vienna naturally became the first object of his attack.

Vercingetorix, at the same time that he despatched an armed force against the Allobroges, endeavoured by means of secret negotiations to win them over by persuasion, trusting to find sufficient sparks of disaffection still alive amongst them to fan into a flame. He failed however to effect an entrance into their territory either by force or negotiation.

But although the Arverne chief failed in his operations against the capital of the Allobroges, he succeeded notwithstanding in cutting off Caesar's communications and supplies from the rest of Provincia and Italy[1].

Finding himself thus isolated, Caesar showed his extraordinary resource by procuring from beyond the Rhine German cavalry and light infantry, of which he stood in desperate need to co-operate with his heavy legionaries. It is to be noted that the crowning victory over Vercingetorix at Alesia was largely attributable to the

[1] *De Bello Gallico*, VII. 65.

prowess of the German cavalry brought over at this crisis[1].

Lying as it does quite outside the limits of this sketch, I am unfortunately debarred from attempting any detailed description of the operations around Alesia—the most interesting episode in Caesar's Gallic Wars.

It is, however, within my province to note that, although the back of the Gallic revolt was broken by the surrender of Vercingetorix, B.C. 52, the fighting was continued and Caesar's presence required in Gaul for about two years longer.

For in B.C. 51, the Roman Province incurred the serious danger of being overrun by a band of some 2000 adventurers and jail-birds, got together by Drappes and Lucterius. This disaster was however averted by the skilful operations of Caninius the legatus, whom Caesar detached for the purpose. The siege and capture of Uxellodunum, the chief oppidum of the Cadurci, by cutting off its water supply—operations conducted by Julius Caesar in person—put an end to the fighting in the South on the borders of the Roman Province. For the Aquitanians surrendered without striking a blow.

After spending a few days at Narbonne dispensing justice and despatching other business with his wonted expedition, Caesar hurried back to Belgium, spending his last winter in Gaul at Nemetocenna[2] (Arras).

The outbreak of the Civil War B.C. 49 occurred most opportunely for the fortunes of Julius Caesar. For it not only furnished military employment for the Roman and Italian army, with which he had subdued Gaul, and which was devoted to him by the closest ties, but also for the restless spirits amongst the Gauls themselves, who might otherwise have broken out into revolt behind his back.

The Legion of the Alaudae (larks), which was en-

---

[1] *De Bello Gallico*, VII. 80.   [2] *Ibid.* VIII. 46.

tirely composed of natives of Gaul, had been incorporated with the Roman army[1] as early as B.C. 55, being equipped in the Roman fashion. It was especially favoured by Caesar, and having rendered him the greatest services, was admitted bodily to Roman citizenship a few years later. Caesar now proceeded to a special enlistment of picked men from all the different states of Gaul[2], whom he had drilled under his own superintendence to be in readiness to follow his Roman legions across the Pyrenees for the encounter with Pompey's lieutenants, Petreius and Afranius, in Spain, which he foresaw was imminent.

But the episode in the Civil War, which especially concerns the Roman Province, of which Domitius Ahenobarbus had been appointed governor by the Senate in succession to Caesar, is unquestionably the siege of Marseilles. If Marseilles had been merely an independent Greek city, its history and fate would be of comparative unimportance to the subject we have in hand. It is, however, necessary to bear in mind that besides being a city, Massilia was an independent Greek state, whose territory extended as far as Monaco eastward and the Pyrenees westward—a stretch of about 300 miles of coast. In addition to this it included all the country comprised between the Rhone and the Cevennes mountains. The occurrence of the name Gretia in the Section of the Table of Peutinger is a proof that its Greek character was preserved by the country between the Rhone and the Durance as late as the age of Theodosius.

That a part of this inland extension of territory was a recent acquisition, dating from Pompey's re-conquest of Provincia about 20 years earlier, we learn incidentally from the statement of their case made to Caesar by the Massiliot envoys in pleading their excuse for wishing

---

[1] Suetonius, *Julius*, 24.
[2] *De Bello Civili*, I. 39. "Nominatim ex omnibus civitatibus nobilissimo et fortissimo quoque evocato."

to remain neutral in the Civil War. The envoys observed, that as they understood the situation, the Roman people was split up into two factions, the respective leaders of which were Cnaeus Pompeius and Caius Caesar,—both patrons of their commonwealth, to the former of whom they were indebted for the public concession of the territories of the Volcae Arecomici and Helvii, and to the latter for attributing to their state increased revenue from the vanquished "Salyes" or Salluvii[1]. That having received equal benefits from both, their proper course seemed to be to show their good will to both by remaining neutral, and receiving neither of them within their city or harbour.

However, while the negotiations were pending between Caesar and the Massiliot envoys, Domitius Ahenobarbus[2], the newly appointed governor of the Provincia Narbonensis (as it may now be convenient to call it, to distinguish it from the rest of Gallia Transalpina) suddenly arrived at Marseilles, with a flotilla of seven swift cruisers from Cosa, a port on the Etrurian coast, and Igilium, an island lying off it.

Notwithstanding that he owed his life and liberty to the magnanimity of Caesar, into whose hands he had been lately delivered by his own troops at Corfinium, Domitius Ahenobarbus did not hesitate to put himself at the head of the sea and land forces which the Massiliots had got together to support the cause of Pompey.

That the leanings of the Massiliots should have been to the side of Pompey and the Senate in spite of their affectation of neutrality, was natural enough. For their Republic was the most conservative and stable known to antiquity, whereas Caesar was the incarnation of the Revolution. In him Sylla had truly remarked there were contained many Mariuses. The governing body

---

[1] *De Bello Civili*, I. 35. "Victos Sallyas" is the emendation of the text proposed by Glandorpius.

[2] Grandson of the first proconsul, maker of the Via Domitia.

of the Massiliots was a council of 600 life-senators, who delegated their powers to a Cabinet of 15, with an inner Cabinet of 3, of whom one was chosen president. It was the Cabinet of 15 who stated their case for neutrality to Caesar.

But the time for negotiation was now passed, and Caesar took his measures accordingly. His first step was to bring up three of his legions for the purpose of investing Marseilles by land; his second was to give orders for the construction of a dozen ships of war at Arles to co-operate with his land forces. Within 30 days from the date of its issue, this order was executed and the ships duly delivered. It would appear from this fact that the city of Arles, with its ship-building facilities, had been retained in Roman hands after Pompey's reconquest of Provence, when it became a centre of Roman roads.

But the war in Spain requiring his immediate presence, Caesar was obliged to relinquish for the present the direction of the operations around Marseilles, and to hurry across the Pyrenees to join the main body of his army and Gallic auxiliaries awaiting him in the basin of the Iberus (Ebro).

The prosecution of the siege operations by land was in the meanwhile entrusted to Caius Trebonius, the legatus left behind by Caesar, while Decimus Brutus (or Decius as he is styled by Shakespeare), was to take the command of the fleet.

## CHAPTER XIV.

### SIEGE AND BLOCKADE OF MARSEILLES.

As the siege of Marseilles is the only military operation in the history of the Roman province connected with the name of Julius Caesar, and as he has himself furnished a minute description of it, this chapter will be devoted to reproducing its main features drawn directly from the text of the *De Bello Civili*, L. II. c. 1—22.

From the present aspect of the city, which stretches over an extensive area, covering the high ground on both sides of the old harbour as well as reaching inland up and beyond the hill of St Charles—the site of the modern railway station—it is hard to realize that the Massilia of the Phocaeans was confined to a peninsula between the old harbour and a creek of La Joliette.

Yet the description of it in the first chapter of the second book of the *De Bello Civili* leaves no doubt on the point. It runs thus. "For Massilia is almost entirely washed by the sea on three sides; it is only approachable by land on its fourth side."

A glance at the plan opposite this page will make this clearer to the reader *on paper*, but it is less easy to trace on the spot the line of ancient wall, which was carried across the neck connecting the peninsula with the line of coast.

In the *Ora Maritima* of Festus Avienus v. 706—708, the situation of Massilia is described as follows:

"Latera gurges adluit,
Stagnum ambit urbem, et unda lambit oppidum
Laremque fusa: *civitas paene insula est.*"

To man the line of their city wall and at the same

time their fleet, the Massiliots called in their former trusty mercenaries, the Albici, who appear to have served the Greek republic in peaceful times as agricultural labourers, and to have been always ready at a moment's notice to respond to a call to arms.

The Albici, whose head-quarters were at Reii (Riez), still a considerable city lying among the hills between the Verdon and the Durance, some fifty miles to the north of Marseilles, were a brave and hardy race, which had always been loyal to their Greek employers. From their readiness to take up arms against their all-powerful neighbours, the Ligurian Salyes, in defence of Marseilles, it seems most probable that the Albici were a tribe of friendly Celts[1] who had been induced to cross the Durance to take service under the Greek republic.

For although, as I stated in my Introductory Chapter, the country south of the Durance was never conquered by Celts, a few isolated Celtic tribes, one of which he calls Commoni, found their way across that river and are mentioned by Pliny as settled in the neighbourhood of Marseilles.

In spite of the representations to Caesar of the desire of the republic of Marseilles to preserve a benevolent neutrality at the outbreak of the Civil War, it soon became clear that the city was thoroughly equipped to stand a siege.

Immense supplies of war material of every kind were found to have been accumulated in readiness for any emergency, and the wall and towers on the land side were provided with exceptionally powerful batteries of 'tormenta'—machines for discharging heavy missiles of metal or stone.

It was a strange turn of Fortune's wheel, that the Romans, to whose benevolent intervention Massilia owed its preservation from being stormed by the Salluvii,

---

[1] The friendly Celts, who are mentioned by Livy as having accompanied the Roman cavalry, sent *en reconnaissance* up the Rhone Valley at the time of Hannibal's invasion, were probably Albici.

should now be laying siege to the city on their own account.

It was a work of months to throw up the embankments required to provide access to the walls over the low ground, and to construct many kinds of complicated shelters to protect the besiegers from the showers of missiles discharged from the tormenta.

While these siege-works, on which gangs of native workmen collected from all parts of Provincia were mainly employed, were being pushed forward, the twelve war-ships ordered by Caesar duly arrived from Arles. As it is expressly stated[1] that only thirty days had elapsed since the felling of the trees of which they were constructed, it is not to be wondered at that they proved somewhat unwieldy.

Having a fleet of seventeen war-ships at his disposal, Domitius Ahenobarbus seems to have considered that they would be advantageously employed in a trial of strength with the twelve unseasoned ships, which appear to have constituted the whole of Caesar's fleet. These twelve ships were placed under the command of Decimus Brutus, who drew them up near the islands lying outside the old harbour.

Never doubting but what he would make short work of them, Domitius bore down triumphantly upon his opponents. For in addition to his war-ships he was reinforced by a number of smaller craft.

Having an insufficient number of sailors available, Caesar, before setting out to join his army in Spain, had called on the three legions left with his legate Trebonius to furnish volunteers to serve on his extemporized fleet. The call was readily responded to and the ships manned by the pick of the legionaries. As it happened, the very unwieldiness of the vessels turned out to be just suited to the unseamanlike character of the crews. For from the heaviness of the newly-felled timber, the vessels built at Arles proved exceptionally

[1] *De Bell. Civ.* 1. 36.

steady, and served as solid stages for fighting a land-battle at sea.

Both men and ships being alike incapable of vying with their Massilian opponents in naval tactics, Caesar's galleys made it their sole aim to get to close quarters as quickly as possible. Once amongst the enemy's ships, the legionaries threw out grappling-irons, with which they held them fast, sometimes catching two at a time, till they had boarded aud despatched their crews composed chiefly of Albici. After sinking three and capturing six of the Massiliot ships, Decimus Brutus returned in triumph to his moorings, while Domitius retired discomfited with only seven ships.

Meanwhile the progress of the siege operations was slow on the land side owing to the difficult nature of the ground, the heavy discharges of masses of rocks from the heights on the heads of the besiegers, and the frequent sorties of the Albici, ever ready to take advantage of the confusion and havoc occasioned by the tormenta in the ranks of the legionaries.

Hearing of the discomfiture of Domitius, and the loss of more than half his ships, Pompey lost no time in despatching his admiral L. Nasidius, then commanding his fleet in Sicilian waters, with sixteen ships of war to the relief of the Massiliots.

When the news of the arrival of this opportune reinforcement reached the ears of the Massiliot population, which had been deeply dejected since witnessing the overthrow of their hopes at sea, their spirits immediately revived, and the whole city was eager for a fresh naval encounter.

It was well for the Massiliots that the second and more decisive sea-fight, on which all their fresh hopes were staked, was destined to come off out of sight of their city. For instead of bringing his ships close up to Marseilles, Nasidius halted them opposite Tauroenta, some 20 miles to the eastward towards Toulon. He seems to have shrunk from the risk of exposing himself to the risk of an attack, before he had effected his junction with Domitius. For with the six war-ships captured from the Massiliots in the late engagement, Decimus Brutus had now a fleet of eighteen vessels, more fully equipped and better fitted to put to sea.

Sending forward a despatch boat to announce his arrival at Tauroenta, Nasidius summoned Domitius to join him there with the ships that remained to him and nine fresh ones, which the Massiliots had equipped to replace those captured.

As it became clear that the combined fleets opposed to him would decline fighting in the waters within sight of the city and in touch with the old harbour, which appears throughout to have been in his possession, Decimus Brutus determined to accept battle at Tauroenta, where Nasidius offered it.

Described as a 'Castellum Massiliensium'[1] Tauroenta is a spot to which M. Lentheric has devoted fifty somewhat uncalled-for pages in the *Riviera Ancient and Modern*, the English rendering of his *Provence Maritime*. As by his own showing on p. 122 'Etiam periere ruinae', I do not feel called upon to add anything to the mention of the name, which only serves to mark the point on the rocky coast of Provence, off which the battle was fought, which put an end to the independence of the Massiliot republic B.C. 49.

To meet Decimus Brutus approaching from the westward with his eighteen vessels, the Pompeian fleet advanced in two divisions, the seventeen Massiliot Greek ships being placed inshore on the right, while the sixteen under the command of Nasidius formed the left wing towards the open sea.

Very different was the spirit which animated them respectively, the Massiliots feeling that all depended on the issue of this supreme occasion, on which they were fighting for their hearths and homes, while the sailors of Nasidius were supremely indifferent. Having no

[1] Caesar, *De Bell. Civ.* II. 4.

material interests at stake and without a spark of patriotic sentiment, for they had no country to defend, the Latin contingent of Nasidius, from which the Massiliots hoped such great things, proved in the simple but expressive words of the text 'of no good at all'. (Nasidianae naves nulli usui fuerant[1].)

As a matter of fact, they bolted at the critical moment of the battle, their crews not being worked up to the pitch of risking their lives on an alien adventure, without any encouragement from fellow countrymen on the spot.

In striking contrast to the unadorned brevity of the text of Caesar's *Civil War* is the account of the sea-fight in Lucan's *Pharsalia*, Book III., of which I give below a specimen—Rowe's well-known version:—

> *Massilia's* navy, nimble, clean, and light,
> With best advantage, seek or shun the fight;
> With ready ease, all answer to command,
> Obey the helm, and feel the pilot's hand.
> Not so the *Romans*; cumbrous hulks they lay,
> And slow and heavy hung upon the sea;
> Yet strong, and for the closer combat good,
> They yield firm footing on th' unstable flood.
> Thus Brutus saw, and to the master cries
> (The master in the lofty poop he spies
> Where streaming the Praetorian ensign flies),
> Still wo't thou bear away, still shift thy place,
> And turn the battle to a wanton chase?
> Is this a time to play so mean a part,
> To tack, to veer, and boast thy trifling art?
> Bring to. The war shall hand to hand be tried,
> Oppose thou to the foe our ample side
> And let us meet like men, the chieftain said;
> The ready master the command obeyed,
> And sidelong to the foe the ship was laid.
> Upon his waist fierce fall the thund'ring Greeks,
> Fast in his timber stick their brazen beaks;
> Some lie by chains and grappling strong compell'd,
> While others by the tangling oars are held;
> The seas are hid beneath the closing war,
> Nor need they cast the jav'lin now from far;

---

[1] *De Bell. Civ.* II. 7.

> With hardy strokes the combatants engage,
> And with keen faulchions deal their deadly rage;
> Man against man, and board by board they lie,
> And on those decks their arms defended die;
> The rolling surge is stained around with blood,
> And foamy purple swells the rising flood."

In spite of the cowardly withdrawal of the ships of Nasidius at the critical moment, the Massiliot vessels by no means lost all hope of victory, but continued to make a good fight of it single-handed. They were however at last obliged to acknowledge their defeat, when five of their vessels were sunk and four captured.

From the camp of Trebonius, on the heights opposite overlooking the city, the Roman soldiers while the sea-fight was in progress could plainly descry crowds of Massiliot women and children thronging the temples and bowing down before the images of their gods in earnest supplication. As soon as it became known that their fleet had been beaten, owing to the flight of Nasidius, whose arrival had only a few days before excited such wild hopes in their breasts, a great wail of grief rent the air. To hear it, any one would have supposed that the city itself had fallen into the hands of the enemy.

But although the Massiliots must have felt that the fate of their city was sealed now that the Romans were as completely masters by sea as by land, they relaxed none of their efforts in defending their walls, against which Trebonius pushed his attack with renewed vigour.

The rocky nature of the soil rendering underground approaches impossible in the absence of explosives, with the use of which the Romans were unacquainted, it was necessary to construct moveable shedding of great strength to protect the advance of the besiegers.

Against these sheds, as they were seen approaching the walls, the besiegers would discharge every available missile and finally roll down huge masses of rock, when they got nearer. If these failed to smash in the roofing, they would hurl down casks filled with burning pitch and lighted torches.

An inexhaustible supply of such material having been accumulated at Marseilles, the best furnished port in the western basin of the Mediterranean, the progress of the siege was slow, no shedding composed of wooden framework filled in with such inflammable material as osiers and hurdles proving fire-proof. At length however after weary months of ineffectual attempts, the besiegers contrived to construct an immensely strong covered approach, 5 ft. high by 4 ft. broad, the stout wooden framework of which was filled in with clay and bricks, and the whole cased in with similar incombustible material.

Approaching by means of this 'musculus' (as Caesar calls it) the principal tower and key of the defences in the city wall, the besiegers succeeded in effectually undermining it and bringing part of it down with a run, thereby causing a formidable breach.

Upon this, the besieged, desisting from further show of resistance, and throwing themselves at the feet of Trebonius, obtained from him the concession of an armistice, pending the arrival of Caesar, whose return from the successful termination of the Spanish War was shortly expected.

However, as Caesar's arrival was unexpectedly deferred, the Massiliots in flagrant violation of the armistice and hoping to find the Romans napping at the hour of noon, suddenly sallied forth through the breach in the walls and attacked them unexpectedly. Availing themselves of a strong wind (probably the Mistral, with which every visitor to the French Riviera is only too familiar), the Massiliots treacherously set fire to everything inflammable in the Roman lines, destroying the bulk of their siege appliances.

As Caesar, shortly before the commission of this treacherous outrage, had sent an express injunction to Trebonius, that he was *on no account* to sanction the storming of the city, the Massiliots escaped the condign punishment which they richly deserved and which the Roman legionaries were with great difficulty withheld from inflicting upon them then and there.

Retiring within the walls and repairing as best they could the breach in their defences, occasioned by the fall of the tower, the Massiliots prepared for further resistance.

The Romans meanwhile on their side zealously set to work at the re-construction of their siege appliances, felling for this purpose all the timber still available in the neighbourhood.

When the siege had been prolonged a considerable time, famine, resulting from the effectual blockade, which had been established by Decimus Brutus since his second naval victory, came to the assistance of the besiegers, bringing all kinds of disease in its train. From this it resulted that on Caesar's arrival, the Massiliots, being unable to hold out any longer, and trusting to his well-known clemency, surrendered their city to him unconditionally. All lives were spared, Domitius Ahenobarbus, afraid to trust himself a second time to Caesar's generosity, having escaped by sea a few days previously to the surrender.

The terms exacted by the conqueror were the surrender of all arms and military engines; of all ships and naval stores; of the whole of the public treasure, and the forfeiture of all territory.

A garrison consisting of two Roman legions was quartered upon the city. From henceforth Marseilles ceased to exist as an independent republic. She was however permitted to elect her civil magistrates and to enjoy the privilege to local self-government.

## CHAPTER XV.

### EVENTS OF THE YEAR FOLLOWING THE ASSASSINATION OF JULIUS CAESAR.

THE last public act of Julius Caesar affecting the Roman Province was the despatch of Tiberius Claudius Nero—the first husband of Livia, and father of Tiberius and Drusus—with fresh batches of Roman colonists, mostly veteran soldiers, to plant new or re-inforce existing colonies in Gaul. Of these only two, Narbonne and Arles, are mentioned by name, but the context[1] expressly implies that there were others besides.

That Frejus was among them can hardly be questioned. For on that 'claustrum Galliae' alone was bestowed the distinction of being called after the conqueror Forum 'Julii.'

From having been at the outset a naval and military station settled amidst a native population, Forum Julii was now raised to the full rank of a Roman Colony. It is first mentioned B.C. 43 (the year following the death of Julius Caesar) in the correspondence of Cicero with Munatius Plancus, Proconsul of Gallia Comata.

To enable the reader to appreciate the importance of the events, of which the Roman Province was now to become the scene, it is necessary to take a general view of the political situation after the disappearance of Julius Caesar from the midst of the Roman world.

Notwithstanding that Caesar was Dictator at the time of his assassination (with Marcus Aemilius Lepidus

---

[1] Suetonius, *Tiberius*, c. 4.

for Master of his Horse), Marcus Antonius and P. Cornelius Dolabella, son-in-law of Cicero, were associated with him as Consuls.

The dictatorship having fallen to the ground, the supreme power in the state devolved upon the Consuls, who at first took opposite sides.

While Marc Antony stood forth as the champion of Caesarism, Dolabella, under the influence of Cicero, maintained the cause of the Senate, which was that of the assassins of Caesar. He even went the length of removing the column and altar, which the partisans of Caesar had erected in the Forum in his honour, and caused those of the intending worshippers on whom he could lay hands either to be hurled from the Tarpeian rock or crucified. Dolabella, however, was shortly after got rid of, accepting as he did the bribe of the proconsulship of Syria, proffered him by Antony.

Meanwhile a more formidable rival to the championship of Caesarism arrived in the person of the young Octavianus, who was pursuing his studies of Greek at Apollonia, when 'the news of his great-uncle's death reached him. On his arrival at Rome, he presented himself before Antony, claiming to be recognised as the testamentary heir of his uncle and father by adoption.

But as Antony had already spent in bribery the bulk of the 4000 talents (about 1 million sterling) which Calpurnia, the widow of Julius Caesar, had handed over to him, as Caesar's relative and representative (for Antony's mother was a Julia), he received Octavianus with such coldness as to drive him into the opposite camp.

Welcomed by Cicero and the party of the Senate, Octavianus proceeded notwithstanding to summon to his standard the veteran soldiers, dispersed all over Italy on farms granted them by his uncle.

When towards the end of the year B.C. 44, Marc Antony, before the expiration of his consulship, left Rome for Gallia Cisalpina with the object of expelling from the governorship of that Province Decimus Brutus, who had been confirmed in his appointment originally made by Caesar himself, Octavianus put himself and his veterans at the disposal of the Senate to lend a hand in putting down Antony.

Invested with the rank of praetor, and acting in concert with the consuls of the year, Aulus Hirtius and Vibius Pansa, Octavianus in the spring of B.C. 43 marched at the head of his veterans into Gallia Cisalpina, where Marc Antony was laying siege to Mutina (Modena), within the defences of which ancient fortress Decimus Brutus had taken refuge.

Although the fighting in the neighbourhood of Mutina resulted in the total defeat of Antony and the consequent relief of Brutus, both consuls by some unfortunate fatality lost their lives in the operations. As their deaths occurred most opportunely for Octavianus, who was known to have coveted the consulship, some suspicion of connivance at their deaths fell upon their youthful associate. When Octavianus subsequently declined to join Decimus Brutus in a vigorous pursuit of Antony, it soon became evident that he had a game of his own to play, which was not that of Cicero and the Senate.

The correspondence of Cicero[1] with the three generals commanding in the three Gallic provinces at the moment of Antony's defeat enables us to follow step by step the events there enacted, which led directly up to the overthrow of the republic. It is a bit of history, which only the light of local colouring can bring into full relief.

Of the three generals ostensibly commanding for the Senate in the Gauls, Decimus Brutus in Gallia Cisalpina, Lucius Munatius Plancus in Gallia Ulterior, and Aemilius Lepidus in Provincia Narbonensis, only the first was a genuine republican. The other two, Plancus and Lepidus, were political trimmers, without any fixed principles, and only bent on finding themselves on the winning

[1] *Epist. ad Fam.* x, xi, *passim.*

side. Both however in their letters made strong professions of their devotion to Cicero and the republic. It would appear that Cicero was deceived by them both, while Decimus Brutus, who distrusted Lepidus from the beginning, continued to believe in the loyalty of Plancus to the last.

Such were the men, on whose decision the future of the republic depended at this important crisis.

Octavianus in the meanwhile kept in the background, intriguing all round, and displaying even at that age—he was not yet turned 20—the remarkable sagacity, for which he was distinguished during his whole career.

The first letter in the series, which sets forth the situation after the defeat and flight of Antony from Modena, is one addressed to Cicero by Decimus Brutus, from the camp Dertona, May 5, B.C. 43.

If the reader will take the trouble to glance at the Map of the Riviera at the beginning of the volume, he will observe that Dertona (Tortona) whence the letter is dated is situated at the junction of two Roman roads—the Via Postumia leading to Genoa, and the Via Aemilia Scauri leading to Savona. Having two days' start of Brutus, Antony had just passed through Dertona on his flight from Modena through Placentia to Vada Sabata.

"I want you to know where that place is," writes Decimus Brutus to Cicero; "It lies at the point of junction of the Alps and Apennines[1] and in a most difficult line of country to march through."

When in B.C. 109, Aemilius Scaurus, the Censor, carried the Etrurian coast-road known as Via Aurelia onwards through Pisae and Luna[2] under the name called from himself 'Aemilia,' he made Vada Sabata its terminus on the coast, though he continued it inland across the Apennines to Dertona.

---

[1] I have given my reasons in a former chapter for placing the junction of the Alps and Apennines elsewhere.

[2] Strabo, p. 217.

The pass over the Apennines behind Vada (Savona) being the lowest to be met with along the entire Riviera, the Romans adopted it in preference to that by way of Genoa, as the main thoroughfare of their communications between Gallia Cisalpina and Liguria. They established a Castra Stativa there, which remained their headquarters on the coast till the time of Augustus.

It was by this pass and this road that Antony had outstripped his pursuers in reaching the coast at Vada, where he was joined by his lieutenant Ventidius with the seventh, eighth and ninth Legions, and by his brother Lucius Antonius, with a force of five thousand cavalry, which had escaped with its entire strength from before Modena.

Dertona, whence the letter of Decimus Brutus is dated, is described by Strabo as "a considerable city (ἀξιόλογος), lying half-way between Genoa and Placentia." The Roman city, at the foot of which the modern Tortona stretches out, was built on heights, forming spurs of the Apennines thrown out towards the Po. It was a strategic position of great importance, being the first of a succession of natural fortresses, thrown out *en échelon* as if to defend the approaches to Placentia from the west.

Between Vada Sabata and Dertona it is still possible to come upon some traces of the inland prolongation of the Via Aemilia Scauri. As no local information is to be got, and the guide books are absolutely silent on the subject, I will endeavour to supply sufficient data to guide the steps of any future traveller who may be tempted to explore the region.

Driving from Savona[1] through its western suburb to Vado, where the tradition of the Roman camp survives in the name Quintana, still retained by one of its streets, you cross the plain to the village of Quiliano, where at the foot of the hills the carriage road ends, and a

[1] Savona, where fair accommodation is afforded at the Albergo Srizzera, will be found the most convenient headquarters for exploring the region.

rough track continues up the valley in a north-easterly direction.

Induced by a preliminary study of the Itinerary of Antonine and the Table of Peutinger to strike the Apennines at Quiliano, I was encouraged to proceed by the easiness of the ascent, and the report that I should shortly come upon traces of three bridges.

In less than an hour, I had encountered the first of the trio. I was however totally unable to judge of its age as it had lately received a thick coating of plaster. Crossing it, I mounted the zig-zags, by which the track is carried onwards up steep and grassy slopes to a higher level, where I was confronted by bridge No. 2 of unmistakeably Roman construction. Although a mere footpath leads up to either end of the bridge, there is a 9 ft. wide roadway still well preserved on the bridge itself. I have no doubt that this determines the passage of the Via Aemilia Scauri.

About half-an-hour further up, the valley divides into two branches, the left hand one having been followed by the Roman road, as is proved by the ruins of bridge No. 3, the massive concrete piers and arches of which have alike collapsed and block up the narrow bed of the stream.

The whole distance from Quiliano at the foot of the Pass to the village of Cadibona on the summit may be accomplished in less than three hours, giving time for examination of the bridges. As Cadibona is on the high road from Savona, a carriage may be sent on to await the traveller there. On the south side of the Apennines I know of nothing but the remains of these bridges to declare the former passage of the Via Aemilia Scauri. On the north side however, between the modern Acqui (Aquae Statiellae) and Tortona, I followed the road itself for at least two miles continuously in the territory of the Commune of Sezze.

Under the name of 'Via Levata' (raised road) it crops up in the plain between the rivers Bormida and

Orba and is carried in a straight line through the crops. Although its crown is uniformly 9 ft. wide and its base a foot or two wider, it appears to be entirely disused and leads nowhere, ending abruptly in a cornfield. I could however distinctly trace the line of its onward course through the standing corn up to the bank of the River Orba, where there is no longer a bridge to carry it over.

There is no sign of pavement left anywhere along the road, which consists of loose stones and gravel, resting on what has proved a practically indestructible substratum of concrete.

There is a commodious and clean Inn at the village of Sezze, which is a convenient centre for visiting the battlefield of Marengo, as well as exploring what remains of the Via Aemilia Scauri.

The 'Sindaco' and the Schoolmaster at Sezze are both obliging and enlightened guides to the honours of the place, and will readily point out the course of the 'Via Levata' through the communal territory.

## CHAPTER XVI.

### MEETING OF ANTONY AND LEPIDUS ON THE RIVER ARGENS.

I HAVE explained in the preceding Chapter that Vada Sabata, where Marc Antony made a brief halt in the permanent camp, was at that time the terminal coast station and inland turning point of the Via Aemilia Scauri. It was his last chance of procuring supplies from a Roman base, on the Italian side of the Maritime Alps, which had never yet been scaled by a Roman army.

But no ordinary depot could have nearly sufficed to meet the extraordinary call now made upon it. Not only had the motley and disorderly crowd now gathered around Antony, consisting of demoralized legionaries, jail-birds and casuals pressed into the ranks during his flight from Modena to the coast, to be provided for, but the three fresh legions brought in by Ventidius and the body of 5,000 cavalry by L. Antonius.

If Antony could have reckoned on being joined by the legions which Ventidius Bassus his able legate had recruited amongst Caesar's veterans and his native Picenates and brought unexpectedly from the shores of the Adriatic into Liguria, he would have been less eager to fill up the ranks of his own legions with such worthless material. At Vada Antony found himself once more at the head of a considerable force, but not of strength sufficient to turn round and face Decimus Brutus, who had arrived at Acqui with 7 legions in pursuit of him.

There was nothing for it then but to continue his flight into Gallia Narbonensis, across the Maritime Alps and the hardly less formidable Esterel mountains lying between the Alps and Forum Julii.

If he could but once reach the Roman Province, Antony fully reckoned on bringing over to his side his old associate Lepidus.

But to attempt to carry an unprovided force of 20,000 infantry and 5,000 cavalry for about 100 miles first along an arid strip of coast, presenting a succession of precipitous headlands, and then over a double range of mountains destitute of food or water-supply, was a task which only a general in desperate circumstances would have undertaken.

Both Pompey and Caesar, when it became necessary to march armies into Gaul over the Alps, deliberately avoided the coast-road.

How Antony and his followers paid desperately for their temerity we read in Plutarch's life[1] of him:—

"Antony, in his flight, was overtaken by distresses of every kind, and the worst of all of them was famine. But it was his character in calamities to be better than at any other time. Antony, in misfortune, was most nearly a virtuous man. It is common enough for people, when they fall into great disasters, to discern what is right, and what they ought to do; but there are but few who in such extremities have the strength to obey their judgment, either in doing what it approves or avoiding what it condemns; and a good many are so weak as to give way to their habits all the more, and are incapable of using their minds. Antony, on this occasion, was a most wonderful example to his soldiers. He, who had just quitted so much luxury and sumptuous living, made no difficulty now of drinking foul water and feeding on wild fruits and roots. Nay, it is related they ate the very bark of trees, and,

---

[1] The extract is from Clough's Edition (Nimmo, 1893).

in passing over the Alps, lived upon creatures that no one before had ever been willing to touch."

That any of the troops which followed Antony and his legate Ventidius Bassus along the Riviera and across the Alps should have survived the terrible ordeal, is harder to understand than that many of them perished in the attempt. For of those who safely achieved the passage of the Alps many must have succumbed, exhausted in the deep gorges of the Esterel, choked as they are with the impenetrable thicket for which that range has always been remarkable. To what extent the passage of the Esterel may have been facilitated by the existence of the road, which the Massiliots were under obligation to construct along the shore, we have no means of judging.

That no classical writer should as much as even mention the name of the Esterel may be taken as a proof that as a rule the Romans gave it a wide berth. The name Esterel is said to be derived from "Sueltri"—a Ligurian tribe marked in the Table of Peutinger above Forum Julii. As I have reminded the reader more than once, Roman armies were in the habit of reaching Forum Julii by sea. But Antony was entirely without ships to carry him even from Monaco, where Roman armies sometimes embarked for Gaul and Spain, after marching so far, as we know that the unfortunate Consul C. Hostilius Mancinus did[1].

The starving and draggled condition of Antony and his followers, as they emerged into the open from the tangled thickets of the Esterel and presented themselves like so many scarecrows at the gates of Forum Julii, can be more readily imagined than described.

The date of Antony's arrival at Forum Julii is fixed by a letter from L. Munatius Plancus to Cicero written in the latter half of May B.C. 43, from the neighbourhood of Grenoble:—

"Antony with the first division of his army reached

[1] Val. Max. I. 6, 7.

Forum Julii on May 15. Ventidius is within 2 days' march of him. Lepidus is encamped at Forum Voconii, a place which is 24 miles from Forum Julii[1]."

A letter from Lepidus himself to Cicero, dated :—

In camp at the Bridge of the Argens May 22, B.C. 43.

(In castris ad Pontem Argenteum XI. Kal. Jun.— A.V.C. 711) M. Lepidus Imp. Iter. Pont. Max. S. D. M. Tullio Ciceroni[2].

"As soon as I heard that Antony, having sent ahead his brother Lucius with part of his cavalry, was making for my province with his army, I broke up my camp at the confluence of the Rhone and Durance and advanced to meet him. Marching without intermission, I came to Forum Voconii, and pitched my camp *beyond* on the banks of the Argens, opposite that of Antony. Ventidius has joined him with 3 legions...He has a large force of cavalry, which is intact, not having been engaged. It is at least 5,000 strong. As far as this war is concerned, I shall not be found wanting either to the Senate, or the Republic."

A fortnight's rest in the fertile plain of Frejus worked a marvellous change in the appearance and condition of the troops, the cavalry finding abundance of the forage for which the place is still noted. With ranks replenished and fitted out afresh the army of Antony and Ventidius proceeded to march up the valley of the Argens to its meeting with Lepidus. It is hardly too much to say, that on the result of that meeting depended the fate of the Roman Republic.

Although Plutarch represents Antony as approaching Lepidus in the garb of a suppliant, with long and disordered hair and beard unshaved since his defeat, it seems highly improbable that so haughty a character as Antony would have condescended to adopt such an

---

[1] Cicero, *Ad Fam.* x. 17.
[2] Cicero, *Ad Fam.* x. 34. The bridge over the Argens is within one mile of the station Les Arcs, where all the expresses stop between Toulon and Cannes.

attitude in the presence of one so immeasurably his inferior as Lepidus. It appears indeed morally certain that from the first there was a complete understanding in both armies that there was to be no fighting. For even supposing that Lepidus had attempted to redeem the pledge he had given to Cicero that he would stand by the Senate and the Republic, it is almost certain that he could not have carried his army with him.

For the feeling in favour of Caesarism was almost as universal in the Roman army at this period as it was in the French army, when Napoleon appealed to it on his escape from Elba in 1815. Perhaps the only convinced republican in the camp of Lepidus was the Senator Laterensis, who was the accredited representative of the Senate and who took his own life at the Pons Argenteus rather than survive what he considered an act of base treachery. His was indeed the only drop of blood which tinged the limpid waters of the Argens.

Meanwhile L. Munatius Plancus, who had been hovering with his army among the spurs of the Basses Alps and had approached within two days' march of Forum Voconii (or Vocontii as it is sometimes written), on hearing of the understanding between Antony and Lepidus thought it prudent to return to Grenoble to await the further turn of events. For it was clear that until Octavianus had definitely declared himself, it would be risky to take a side. He had besides to reckon with the determined attitude of Decimus Brutus, who lay with his army of seven legions at Eporedia (Ivrée) at the foot of the Little St Bernard, ready at any moment to cross the Alps and hold him true to his pledge to the Republic.

It was not long however before it became clear to Munatius Plancus that it would be agreeable to Octavianus that he should abandon Cicero and the senatorial party, and throw in his lot definitely with that of Antony and Lepidus. He accordingly joined his forces to theirs.

For in the month of August, B.C. 43, Octavianus, having got himself elected Consul with Quintus Pedius, for his colleague, succeeded in passing a law styled 'Lex Pedia,' which declared all the murderers of his uncle Julius Caesar to be outlaws.

Amongst these was Decimus Brutus, whose position in Gallia Cisalpina now became desperate. For the combined armies of Antony Lepidus and Plancus threatened to bear down upon him from Gaul beyond the Alps, while Octavianus, who was commissioned to put the 'Lex Pedia' into execution, was marching towards the Po valley from the South.

Worse than all, he could no longer rely on the loyalty of the majority of his legions. There was nothing then left for Decimus Brutus but to make an attempt to join his fellow outlaw Marcus Brutus in Macedonia. He was however waylaid at Aquileia at the foot of the Julian Alps, and put to death by order of Antony.

Meanwhile, the decrees which had been passed by the Senate acting under the influence of Cicero earlier in the year declaring Antony and Lepidus enemies of their country had been duly repealed before Octavianus effected his junction with them at Bononia.

It was on an island in the river now called the Reno, which flows into the Po beyond Bologna, that the meeting took place, which resulted in the appointment of C. Caesar (Octavianus), M. Antonius, and M. Lepidus as a Triumvirate for regulating the affairs of the Republic for a period of five years (Reipublicae constituendae per quinquennium).

It is notorious that the first act of this body was to agree upon a list of victims, each of the Triumvirs besides handing over their respective enemies to the executioner obliging their colleagues by the sacrifice of some personal friend or relative.

Cicero, who had been the mouth-piece of the Senate and by the recent delivery of his Philippics had rendered himself especially obnoxious to the vindictiveness of Antony, was amongst the first to pay the death penalty.

The head of the illustrious orator and his right hand

were severed from his body by orders of Antony, and affixed to the Rostra, the scene of so many of his former triumphs. It is related that Fulvia the wife of Antony ran a gold pin through the dead orator's tongue.

In the apportionment of their respective spheres of government amongst the Triumvirs, Gaul was assigned to Antony, as one of his provinces. He does not however appear to have ever resided there, preferring the charms of Cleopatra and the luxuries of an Oriental life.

It was reserved for Augustus, after the defeat of his rival at the battle off Actium B.C. 31, to organize finally the administration of the Gallic provinces.

While Lyons (Lugdunum) became the Roman capital of Gallia Comata, the Provincia Narbonensis was administered separately from the rest of Gaul, at first by Augustus and afterwards by the Senate.

It was never Gallic at heart, the Provincials having shown more sympathy with the rebellion of Sertorius in Iberia than with that of Vercingetorix in Gaul. It was at Lugdunum that the representatives of the 60 'civitates' of Gallia Comata met, under the presidency of an elected High Priest, to worship at the famous altar of Augustus and Rome, which competed successfully with Druidism.

The colossal monument erected in honour of Augustus at Turbia commemorates his final victory over the Alpine tribes (B.C. 12), and the opening up of a safe road to traders over the Maritime Alps, which, as so recently conquered, were placed under the orders of a Prefect, directly appointed by the Emperor.

## CHAPTER XVII.

### VIA AURELIA.

Section 1: Aurelia proper.   Section 2: Aemilia Scauri.

"*Via Aurelia.* A Roma per Tusciam et Alpes Maritimas Arelatum usque M. P.[1] DCCXCVII."

Such is the title of the Road following for the most part the shore of the Mediterranean, from Rome to Arles, which is found in the Itinerary of Antonine—the sole official document known to us which contains a complete list of the names of the main roads of the Roman Empire.

While the Itinerary of Antonine is in the shape of a small volume giving the names of the roads, and of the Post Stations, with the distances between each, the Table of Peutinger takes the form of a map, disproportionately compressed from North to South, and elongated from East to West to suit the greater extension of the Roman Empire in that direction. The specimen of one of the twelve sections of the Table of Peutinger shown at the end of the volume will give the reader an idea of its quaint archaic character.

I do not propose here to go at any length into the question of the origin and authenticity of the two abovenamed documents, which, together with the mile-stones which remain, constitute the main source of our information on the subject of Roman Roads. I shall confine

---

[1] The Roman mile was about 100 yards shorter than the English, measuring 1666 yards. It consisted of 1000 paces—the Roman "passus" being 5 ft., *i.e.* the space from the raising up to the setting down of the *right* foot.

myself to giving the general conclusions arrived at, namely that both documents are of a post-Constantine age, probably executed during the reign of Theodosius the Great, though based upon fragments of earlier geographical attempts to depict the Roman world.

The existence of the name Constantinopolis and some others having Christian associations, found in both documents, may be accepted as sufficient proof that they were at all events corrected up to a date, when the Roman world had become Christian.

While the originals of the Itinerary of Antonine and the Table of Peutinger are entirely lost, they are only known to us in careless and corrupt copies of a comparatively late age. Although these copies corroborate each other in the main, marked discrepancies are often found in the distances given by the two documents between the same Stations on the same roads.

While the Itinerary of Antonine limits itself to an enumeration of the main roads, the Table of Peutinger gives besides branches and short cuts (compendia) not to be found in the former document. And this especially applies to the case of the Via Aurelia, the course of which as given in both documents I now propose to consider in some detail. Having devoted portions of ten or more winters to the exploration of the road itself, wherever it can still be traced between Vada Volaterrana and Arles—a distance of about 400 miles—and having besides carefully collected whatever rays of light can be thrown upon the subject by classical and modern writers, I hope I shall not exhaust the patience of my readers by dwelling on it here at some length.

For the Via Aurelia will be found to form a convenient and interesting thread for the traveller to follow up for the whole length of his journey from Arles to Rome or vice versa. In its Roman and international character, the Via Aurelia recognizes no frontiers, and connects the French and Italian Rivieras by an indissoluble bond.

## CHAP. XVII.

Numerous as are the treatises dealing with the various sections of the Via Aurelia, there is not a single one in any language, which treats of it at all adequately as a whole. Even Mommsen has dealt with it in a fragmentary way. For although everything that is known about it is to be found in his monumental work, the *Corpus Inscriptionum Latinarum*, the references to the Via Aurelia are scattered over three separate volumes of about 1000 pages each, and sometimes occur under most unexpected headings, such for instance as Clastidium, Vol. V. Part 2, p. 828. To unearth them and piece them together is no light task.

In his *Provence Maritime* and its English translation *The Riviera, Ancient and Modern*, the pages of M. Lentheric abound in references to the section of the Via Aurelia which lies through French territory, while its onward course along the Italian Riviera is almost entirely ignored. But, even within that limited area, where at all events he ought to be at home, M. Lentheric has fallen into the unaccountable error of attributing the authorship of this section to an Aurelius Cotta, who was consul B.C. 119[1]. For the name of the Via Aurelia is unquestionably derived from a much earlier Aurelius— in all probability the Aurelius Cotta, who was censor B.C. 241. There is however unfortunately no classical text to cite as positive proof of this fact, which has been accepted since the time of Bergier, whose great work, *Les grands Chemins de l'Empire Romain*, was published nearly three centuries ago.

Passing out of Rome through the Porta Aurelia, the original section of the Via Aurelia was carried through Forum Aurelii, as far as Vada Volaterrana on the Etrurian coast—the port of the famous fortress Volaterrae, which itself crowns a lofty ridge, at least 20 miles inland.

The explanation of the Roman road being called Aurelia in Provence is to be found in the fact that the name Aurelia, under which the coast road started from

[1] *Riviera, Ancient and Modern*, p. 22.

Rome and which was confined originally to its first section, was subsequently transferred to the whole length of the road from Rome to Arles. In our own day on the same principle main lines of railway swallow up the subsidiary names, under which their successive sections were known at first.

It was then a quite gratuitous mistake on the part of M. Lentheric to press into his service a later Aurelius, who had nothing whatever to do with Provence or road-making. The first road-maker there, as I have explained above, was Domitius Ahenobarbus, and the original name of the Provençal section of the Via Aurelia was "Via Domitia."

Hirschfeld, however, the author of Vol. XII. of the *Corpus Inscriptionum Latinarum*, which deals with Gallia Narbonensis, declines to apply the name "Aurelia" to the section in question at any period of its existence, in spite of the fact that the Provençal name "lou camin Ourelian" has been applied to it by the peasantry from time immemorial[1]. I venture however to differ from that very high authority. For, in my judgment formed after much intercourse with the natives in all parts of Provence, the Roman roads which connect Frejus with Aix by a single line, and Aix with Arles by two branches, forming a loop passing through Marseilles and Salon respectively, are both entitled to the use of the name "Aurelia." I base my opinion on long established usage, corroborated by the mention of the name in the Itinerary of Antonine.

Although the two quarto volumes of Nicholas Bergier of Rheims are full of erudition conveyed in a delightful form on the construction and administration of Roman roads in general, they unfortunately contain little direct information about any particular road. All that we get from Bergier in addition to the statement that Aurelius Cotta (censor B.C. 241) "donna son nom et son commencement" to the Via Aurelia is the quaint but not

---

[1] *C. I. L.*, Vol. XII. p. 634.

## CHAP. XVII.

very instructive observation "Ce n'est pas toutefois, qu'Aurelius, qui lui a donné son commencement, l'ait conduite jusqu'à Arles. Il a esté continué par plusieurs d'autres jusqu'à dedans la Gaule Narbonnaise *sans perdre son nom.*"

So far from it being a fact that the coast road was carried onwards to Arles without ever losing its original name "Aurelia," we have the well known and undisputed text of Strabo[1] to prove that on its first continuation through Pisae into Liguria the road was called "Aemilia," after Aemilius Scaurus, the author of its prolongation to Vada Sabata[1].

That Strabo should have omitted to mention the name of the exact point, whence Aemilius Scaurus carried his road forward, is most unfortunate. We have however the authority of Mommsen for fixing it at Volaterrae, by which he means of course Vada Volaterrana. For it is impossible to believe that the coast road would have been carried up hill 20 miles out of its way. In Vol. v. part 1, of the *Corpus Inscriptionum Latinarum*, we read at p. 885: "a Volaterris, ubi finem Aureliae caputque Aemiliae fuisse crediderim."

A Roman milestone, which I saw myself in the present year (1898) in the Campo Santo at Pisa, bears in clearly cut letters of the best period the name

VIA AEMILIA

A Roma M. P. CLXXXVIII.

proving that the coast road, at a date not specified on it, bore the name Aemilia at the distance of 188 miles from Rome. As Vada Volaterrana is about 175 miles from Rome the coast road may have borne the name "Aurelia" up to that point, becoming Aemilia beyond it.

For when we come to consider the Julia Augusta section of the coast road, we shall find that the milestones bearing its name are marked at the same time

---

[1] Strabo, p. 217, "ὁ Σκαῦρος...ὁ καὶ τὴν Αἰμιλίαν ὁδὸν στρώσας διὰ Πισῶν καὶ Λούνης μέχρι Σαβάτων κἀντεῦθεν διὰ Δέρθωνος."

with the total of the distance from the capital, notwithstanding that the road changed its name twice in its continuation to Rome over the Via Aemilia Lepidi and the Via Flaminia.

That the coast road bore the name of Aurelia for a considerable distance from Rome is proved by the mention of it in the XIIth Philippic[1], where Cicero refers to it, when declining the proposal that he should repair to Mutina as one of the envoys to treat with Antony when he was laying siege to that place.

"Tres viae sunt ad Mutinam....A supero mari Flammia, ab infero Aurelia, media Cassia."

Further proof of the extension of the Via Aurelia is given by a passage in the life of the Emperor Aurelian by Vopiscus. "Etruriae per Aureliam usque ad Alpes maritimas ingentes agri sunt." This text alone seems to prove that the name Aurelia was applied to the coast road up to the Maritime Alps in the reign of the Emperor Aurelian, A.D. 270—275.

Section No. 2 or Via Aemilia Scauri section of the coast road was about 165 Roman miles in length, its important stations being Pisa, Luna, and Genoa, the last of which is unaccountably omitted by Strabo. From Luna it was carried some considerable distance inland up the valley of the Magra to avoid the precipitous coast between Spezia and Moneglia, where (as I explained in Chap. VI) it was again brought down to the shore. In its onward course through Sestri Levante to Genoa, it sometimes followed the coast, at others kept a mile or two inland. Traces are to be found of its passage at Riva, where the remains of Roman brickwork may be seen on the edge of the stream about 300 yards from its mouth.

Between Rapallo and Ruta the Strada Romana, under which name alone it is known to the natives, may still be followed for an unbroken stretch of three or four miles. It is paved throughout and forms an inland short-

[1] XII. 9.

cut and pleasant alternative to following the windings of the modern high road.

The Strada Romana is hardly ever practicable for wheeled traffic, being often very steep and slippery, after the manner of Roman roads. It offers the great advantage of being cool, moist and shady at all times, and is in strong contrast to the dusty high road, which however commands wider views. The road is the usual width of Roman roads, the pavement measuring about 8 ft., being the regulation width laid down by an ancient law of the Twelve Tables.

I am disposed to believe that much of the pavement which consists of pebbles laid edgeways is Roman. For the large polygonal blocks, with which the roads were paved in towns, were seldom or never used for country roads.

In the Communes of Quinto and Quarto, formerly Roman Stations, five and four miles respectively distant from Genoa, the thread of the Strada Romana can be picked up again and followed for at least half-an-hour's most interesting walk. Here again it lies inland from the dusty or muddy (as the case may be) but always noisy high road, which follows the shore.

In the Commune of Quarto, the Strada Romana is carried over the river Stura by a bridge mainly of Roman construction, the pebbled road being 10 ft. wide in the centre of the bridge. Immediately beyond the bridge, the road winds up the steep and rocky slope to gain the high ground, over which Genoa extends.

Between Genoa and Vada Sabata (now Vado, a suburb of Savona) no further trace of the Via Aemilia Scauri is to be found along the coast, so far as I am aware. I have already treated of its inland continuation to Dertona.

It remains for me to explain in the next chapter the course of the Via Julia Augusta, constructed by Augustus B.C. 12 to fill up the gap on the coast between Vada Sabata and the Var, which was still without a regular Roman road, and unprovided with post stations.

# CHAPTER XVIII.

## VIA AURELIA.

### Section 3: Julia Augusta.

THE construction by Augustus B.C. 12 of the Via Julia Augusta between Vada Sabata and the Var (about 93 miles in length) served at the same time to prolong both the inland Trans-Apennine section of the Via Aemilia Scauri and its coast section (afterwards Via Aurelia) to the Var.

The section of the Julia Augusta between Vada and the Var was therefore the only portion of that road which Augustus had to make entirely new. For the rest of its course between Placentia (the Trebia) and Vada Sabata he had only to improve parts of two roads previously existing. The entire course of the Via Julia Augusta was thus made up:

|   |   | Roman miles. |
|---|---|---|
| (1) | Part of the Via Postumia repaired from Placentia to Dertona | 52 |
| (2) | Part of the Via Aemilia Scauri repaired from Dertona to Vada | 79 |
| (3) | Section of the Via Julia Augusta made new from Vada to the Var | 93 |
|   |   | 224 |

The course of the Via Julia Augusta is fortunately determined for us by the inscription on one of its mile-

CHAP. XVIII. 171

stones found in the Valley of Laghet, one mile to the westward of the monument of Turbia. It is identical with the Via Aurelia in its course along the coast, between Vada and the Var, and only dropped its original name—Julia Augusta—when it became absorbed by the Aurelia of the Antonine Itinerary, as was the case with the Via Aemilia to the east of it, and the Via Domitia to the west.

In making two distinct roads of the Aurelia and Julia Augusta, M. Lentheric is undoubtedly wrong. Had he taken the trouble to study the *Corpus Inscriptionum Latinarum* or the inscriptions on the numerous milestones to which he vaguely alludes as found in the territory of Nice[1], he would have avoided the error into which he has fallen of prefixing to his *Riviera, Ancient and Modern* a map showing the Via Julia Augusta branching from the Aurelia at Turbia and leading from Vence to Frejus by Auribeau. When Augustus carried his Via Julia Augusta over the Alps at Turbia, there was no Via Aurelia to branch off from, nor at any later period, as there never was but one Roman road there at any time. For the later Roman road to Vence (Vintium) branched off the Aurelia at Antibes.

The milestone which decisively determines the direction of the Via Julia Augusta is one of the three with which the visitor is confronted immediately on entering the Municipal Library at Nice. It is numbered 8,102, and is entered, Vol. v. Pt. 2, p. 955 of the *Corpus Inscriptionum Latinarum*[2] amongst the 26 milestones therein numbered from 8083 to 8109 inclusive as belonging to the Via Julia Augusta. That road is described by Mommsen as leading

"Placentiâ Vada, Vadis ad Varum," *i.e.* from Placentia (synonymous with the river Trebia, there forming its

---

[1] *Riviera, Ancient and Modern*, p. 24.
[2] Vol. v. in two parts can be inspected at the Municipal Library.

junction with the Po) to Vada (Sabata) and from Vada to the Var. The inscription runs:

ccxVI
IMP. CAESAR. DIVI
TRAJANI PARTHICI FILIUS
DIVI NERVAE N. TRAJA-
-NUS HADRIANUS AUG
PONT. MAX. TRIB. POTEST. IX
COS. III *VIAM JULIAM
AUG*. A FLUMINE TREB
BIA, QUAE VETUSTATE
INTERCIDERAT, SUA
PECUNIA RESTITUIT
DCV.

The number ccxVI, at the top, gives the distance of that milestone from the 'Trebbia,' while that at the bottom, DCV, shows the total mileage from Rome by the circuitous route *via* Placentia and Rimini, the Julia Augusta having, so to speak, running powers onwards to Rome, over the Via Aemilia Lepidi and the Via Flaminia. The smaller letters in the number ccxVI are not decipherable in the original inscription, but Mommsen has supplied them on the convincing ground that another milestone (No. 8095), which stood four miles nearer the Trebbia, is found inscribed CCXII at the top and DCI at the bottom.

In Vol. v. Part 2, p. 828, Mommsen gives the following table of the composition of the inland circuitous route from Rome to the Var, which Augustus adopted in preference to the coast road, in spite of its being about 200 miles longer:

|  |  |  |  |  |
|---|---|---|---|---|
|  | Via Flaminia. Roma Ariminum | m. p. c. | | CCXXI |
|  | ,, Aemilia Lepidi. Arimino Placentiam | ,, | | CLXVIII |
| Julia | ,, Postumia. Placentia Dertonam | ,, | | LII |
| Augusta | ,, Aemilia Scauri. Dertona Vada | | | LXXIX |
|  | ,, Strata ab Augusto. Vadis ad Varum A. V. C. 742 (B. C. 12) | | | XCIII |
|  | | fiunt m. p. circiter | | DCXIII |

Augustus apparently considered that the alternately swampy and precipitous nature of the coast between Rome and Genoa rendered the effective maintenance of a reliable thoroughfare along the shore an impossibility. The Via Aurelia of the Antonine Itinerary, which attempted it for a time, became practically impassable, as early as the beginning of the 5th century of our era. We gather this from the following passage in the charming poem of Rutilius Numantianus, describing his return journey from Rome to his native Gaul in the reign of the Emperor Honorius. In it, he explains that he preferred the risks of the sea to those of the land route :—

> "Electum pelagus : quoniam terrena viarum
> Plana madent fluviis, cautibus alta rigent :
> Postquam Tuscus ager, postquamque Aurelius agger
> Perpessus Geticas ense vel igne manus,
> Non silvas domibus, non flumina ponte cohercet :
> Incerto satius credere vela mari."

In the age of Dante, the coast road between Lerici (on the bay of Spezia) and Turbia had become proverbial for its impracticability :

> Tra Lerici et Turbia, la più diserta,
> La più romita via, è una scala
> Verso di quella, agevole ed aperta.
>
> Il Purgatorio III. 49[1].

It was necessary, in order to unravel the complications of the Via Aurelia, to explain the course of the Via Julia Augusta, the coast section of which enters into its composition. If, however, one follows the course of the Via Aurelia as laid down by the Itinerary of Antonine, in its entirety, one would also have to include as "Coast-road," or Aurelia, the part of the inland course of the Julia Augusta as far as Dertona and thence back to Genoa by the Via Postumia. But this would be

---

[1] 'Twixt Lerici and Turbia, the most desert,
The most secluded pathway is a stair
Easy and open, if compared with that.

*Longfellow's Translation.*

obviously absurd, as the essential feature of the Via Aurelia (viz. "coast-road") would be lost and the distance from Vada to Genoa, 28 miles by the coast, would be increased to 130.

In my opinion we are justified in declining to follow this aberration of the Itinerary, which is to be ascribed to an error of the copyist, for whom the intricate nature of the whole subject provides some excuse.

It seems much more reasonable to adopt the short cut or compendium indicated by the Table of Peutinger. Such an error goes a long way to explain the exaggeration in the impossible total 797 miles, given in the heading of the Via Aurelia of the Itinerary as the distance from Rome to Arles, which is really about 600 miles by rail *via* Vintimiglia and Marseilles.

Between Vada Sabata and the Var, the thread of the Via Julia Augusta may still be picked up at not unfrequent intervals. It sometimes followed the shore and was sometimes carried a mile or more inland. It was carried over the marshy ground to the east of Albenga, partly on a raised causeway, and partly on arches, which for a length of nearly 200 yards are still extant, forming a striking monument of Roman solidity now known by the name of 'Ponte Lungo.'

Between Albenga and Alassio the Roman road forms one of the most charming walks on the whole Riviera, being carried under olive groves round the shoulder of the mountains for about four miles at a considerable height above the sea, of which it commands glorious views.

On both sides of the picturesque bridge, partly Roman and partly mediaeval, at Andora, the Strada Romana may again be traced, as it crosses the wide valley. Between Diano Marina and Oneglia, the Roman road is (I believe) identical with the steep winding track overhanging the sea, which is much to be recommended to pedestrians, as forming a picturesque short cut between the above-named places.

## CHAP. XVIII.

From Bordighera to Vintimiglia, the Strada Romana runs parallel with the sea, about a thousand yards inland, past the chapel of St Roche, which displays a Roman entablature let into an angle of the wall.

The passage of the road through Vintimiglia is attested by three milestones preserved in the disused church of San Michele—a most picturesque edifice, on the extreme northern edge of the precipitous promontory, on which the now dismantled fortress is built [1].

Between Vintimiglia and Mentone, as all the world knows, the Via Julia Augusta is to be seen in all its naked simplicity, as it is carried over the rocks as you approach along the coast those modern gardens of the Hesperides where the Commendatore Hanbury delights to exercise much appreciated hospitality.

As the Roman road rounds the corner of the Red Rocks (Balze Rosse) famous for its cave dwellings, where prehistoric human skeletons may still be seen *in situ*, its narrow proportions are proved by the 7 ft.—8 ft. wide ledge *chiselled* out of the rock for its passage.

In a narrow roadway winding through the western end of Mentone, the Strada Romana may again be recognized and followed across low-lying orchards before it scales the high ground, overlooking the Cap Martin, where the Roman Station of Lumone was situated.

Crossing the col, which separates the bay of Mentone from that of Monaco, the Via Julia Augusta sweeps round the foot of the village of Roquebrune, whence it mounts by an ascent, nowhere difficult, to Turbia distant six miles from Lumone. It is a walk strongly to be recommended and quite within the compass of an

[1] In his Storia de Vintimiglia, sold at the "Drogheria" in the main street of the Upper Town in the absence of a bookseller's shop, Signor G. Rossi cites a letter from Caelius to Cicero bemoaning his bad luck in being sent to Vintimiglia amidst the snows of the Alps at Christmas time to quell a riot occasioned by the assassination by adherents of Pompey of one of their citizens for having entertained Julius Caesar on his way to Spain at the outset of the Civil War. This as far as I know is the solitary classical text referring to the presence of Julius Caesar on the Riviera.

ordinary pedestrian, starting as the case may be either from Mentone or Monte Carlo, and using the funicular railway at whichever end is most convenient.

In its descent from La Turbie (the Alpe Summa of the Antonine Itinerary) towards the Var, the Via Julia Augusta entirely avoided the difficulties and dangers encountered in the carrying of the Cornice road along the face of the precipices behind Eze. It turned off the main road, about half a mile from the monument of Augustus, to the right down the valley of Laghet, which offers an easy and inviting short cut to Cimiez—the Roman Cemenelum—by La Trinité in the valley of the Paillon. For the Romans were making for Cimiez, avoiding the Greek town of Nice, which remained dependent on Marseilles after the establishment of the Roman Empire, as Strabo informs us[1].

It is surprising how little attention has been paid to the valley of Laghet, which must have served from the earliest times as the main thoroughfare between Italy and Gaul. With their practical eye, the Romans seized on it at once, as a natural opening ready made for their road.

While the distance from Turbia to Cemenelo is only nine miles by the valley of Laghet, it must be nearly 20 by the circuitous route of the Cornice, where a road never existed before the time of Napoleon[2]. In carrying his Via Aurelia by the Cornice, as a separate road from the Julia Augusta, M. Lentheric was clearly in error, as I have already pointed out.

Neither the Itinerary of Antonine, nor the Table of Peutinger shows more than one road, which avoiding Nice, as a Greek settlement, made straight for Cimiez by the valley of Laghet. Nine of the 26 milestones

---

[1] Strabo, IV. Cas. 184, ἡ μὲν Νικαία ὑπὸ τοῖς Μασσαλιώταις μένει καὶ τῆς ἐπαρχίας ἐστίν.

[2] The rough track forming a short cut from Riquier to Villefranche is probably all that remains of the old Greek road, which was bound to keep near the shore.

## CHAP. XVIII.

belonging to the Via Julia Augusta noted by Mommsen were discovered in the valley of Laghet, whereas not a single one has ever been found on the Cornice road.

The modern road, leading to the famous monastery of Laghet, branches off from the Cornice road within half a mile of the village of La Turbie, and the Via Julia Augusta in its turn again branches off from the modern Laghet road a few hundred yards further on, being cut along the face of Monte Sembola. It is only traceable now as a road as far as a quarry, about half a mile from its bifurcation from the modern road, which descends the hill to the monastery.

Beyond the quarry, the Via Julia Augusta becomes a mere footpath, and so continues, till it is lost amongst terraced patches of cultivation on the slopes of Monte Sembola. The milestone represented on the opposite page is still *in situ*, although the road has collapsed entirely. This illustration is from a drawing made by Sir James Harris, the British Consul at Nice, to whom I am much indebted for conducting me to the spot.

The inscription on the milestone proves that it is one of those originally placed there in the reign of Augustus, as his name is still quite legible on it as well as the distance from Rome, DCVII miles. It is numbered 8105 in the Corpus[1].

On a later occasion, when we revisited the valley of Laghet together, I was fortunate enough to find and draw the attention of Sir James Harris to another Roman milestone *in situ*, which had escaped his observation. It is distant exactly one Roman mile from Turbia and marked DCV from Rome.

This milestone appears to be a duplicate, as far as the mileage from Rome is concerned, of that presented by Sir John Boileau to the Municipal Library of Nice,

---

[1] The words "Tribunicia Potestate," of which the initial letters are wanting on the milestone opposite, would supply a clue to its date, if followed, as they usually are, by a number, indicating the number of times the emperor in question had been invested with the tribuneship.

the inscription on which I have quoted above in full. But the milestone DCV still *in situ* is one of those originally set up by Augustus, whereas that in the Municipal Library marks the restoration of the Via Julia Augusta by Hadrian. It is numbered 8101 in the Corpus, where the inscription is given.

It was a common practice of Roman Emperors to place milestones referring to their own work of reparation by the side of those of their predecessors. Three of the nine milestones discovered between Turbia and Cimiez are duplicates, in the sense of marking the same total of miles from Rome.

Besides the nine having inscriptions of some kind, there are several other half-milestones which may or may not be *in situ*. Other fragments have been built into terrace walls,—one of which I examined in the company of the British Consul and Vice-Consul.

To excuse himself for breaking up a milestone which he found on his ground, a peasant-owner remarked to us that there was no object now in maintaining records whole, since the territory around Nice had been transferred from Italy to France in 1860.

No spot in Europe has proved so rich in yield of Roman milestones as the valley of Laghet, and yet it is still uncertain at what point the Via Julia Augusta crossed the Paillon to mount up to Cimiez.

## CHAPTER XIX.

## VIA AURELIA (*continued*).

### Sections 4 and 5.

THAT the original constructors of the first road used by the Romans beyond the Alps, *i.e.* from the Var onwards into Gaul, were the Massiliots about the year B.C. 154, I have already explained, and at the same time pointed out that the Massiliot road could only have been of use to the Romans as far as Forum Julii, because it there branched off to the southward, being under the obligation of keeping within a mile and a half of the sea.

It seems therefore right to call Section 4 of the Via Aurelia from the Var to Forum Julii after its original constructors, 'Via Massiliensis.' That it was taken in hand and utilized by Augustus as a continuation of the Julia Augusta is however proved by a milestone bearing his name, of which I shall say more further on.

But from the absence on any of the milestones discovered westward of the Var of any reference to the total distance in miles either from Rome, or from the Trebia, Section 4 cannot be considered as belonging to the Italian system of roads, which stopped at the Var in the time of Augustus. It was at a much later period that frontiers were ignored by the Via Aurelia.

When we come to consider Section 5 more in detail, I shall be able to adduce proof that Forum Julii was the 'Caput' of that section.

The course of the Massiliot or No. 4 Section of the Via Aurelia from the Var westwards was, as far as Cannes, as nearly as possible identical with the modern high road, which runs parallel to the railway, along the shore. The two Roman milestones, inscribed respectively with the names of Tiberius and Constantine, which are now placed side by side at the foot of the staircase of the Hotel de Ville of Vallauris, were both transported there from the side of the high road, where they originally stood. But, as might be expected, all traces of the Roman road itself have been obliterated by the modern highway constructed on the top of it.

As I observed in the previous Chapter, it was at Antibes that the Roman road (Via Vintiana) branched off from the Aurelia to Vence (Vintium), whence it was carried further inland to "Ad Salinas" (Castellane). Several milestones have been discovered beyond Vence, of which full particulars are given in *Les Inscriptions de Vence* by M. Bourguignat, and in Vol. XII. of the *Corpus Inscriptionum Latinarum*.

Carried through the centre of Cannes, on a higher level than the railway, past la Chapelle St Nicholas, the Via Aurelia, no longer identical with the main thoroughfare, is carried over the insignificant bed of the Riou by the Pont Romain, at the foot of La Croix de Garde. In the steep winding track, which from the bridge may be followed for at least two miles across the ridge of La Croix de Garde till it becomes again obliterated by the broad road-way of a modern boulevard, it requires considerable experience of Roman roads to recognize the famous Via Aurelia.

On its descent from La Croix de Garde, the road was carried over the plain of Laval past the isolated hillock of St Cassien (Arluc, Ara-luci) on the raised causeway along which the modern high road passes.

As the Station, 'Ad Horrea,' has to be fixed at some point 12 Roman miles to the west of Antipolis, and 17 or 18 (according to the Table or Itinerary respectively) to the East of Forum Julii, there is little doubt that it should be identified with Napoule, which agrees with this double condition of distances, and where remains of extensive granaries have been discovered.

At no other point in its course along the coast can the Greek traders of Marseilles have encountered more formidable obstacles to the passage of their road than in carrying it over the jagged porphyry promontories, which descend into the sea from the Esterel mountains between Napoule and Agay.

That they succeeded however in keeping, as they were bound, near the coast, is proved by a milestone found on the road, where it passed round the base of the "Sainte Baume"—the name by which the landward face of the Cap Roux is locally known.

This milestone[1], which stood midway between the Station Ad Horrea and Forum Julii, as is proved by the number VIIII engraved at its base, is inscribed with the name of Augustus, proving that he utilized the Massiliot or Greek road for a time, pending the construction of the more convenient Roman road, which crossed the Esterel by what is now known as the old road to Cannes on the north side of the range.

Several milestones, two of which are preserved in the Museum at Frejus, have been discovered on the Roman rectification of the course of the Massiliot road. One of these states that the Emperor Nero restored the rectification, proving that it was carried out considerably before his time—either by Augustus himself or by Tiberius.

Entering Forum Julii by the Porta Romana, of which the stately double archway was still standing in

---

[1] This milestone was rescued from oblivion by the author, who finding it in two pieces cast away in an abandoned cemetery, had it put together and set up in the esplanade at St Raphael.

the beginning of the last century, the Roman road, afterwards Via Aurelia, formed the main thoroughfare of the city, passing out of it at the Porta Gallica[1].

Whether the original Massiliot road also entered Forum Julii at the point where the Porta Romana was afterwards erected, it is not easy to determine. It is probable, however, that it did not issue from the walls by the Porta Gallica, but by a lower gate facing south and nearer the shore. Here, however, we part company with it.

That Forum Julii was the Caput of Section 5 of the Via Aurelia is proved by the numbering of the miles on a milestone originally found on the Via Aurelia at Camp-Dumy, and now standing in a sheltered corner, outside the parish church of the adjacent village of Cabasse (Matavone).

The milestone in question is one of the series erected by the Emperor Constantine the Great. It is numbered 5470 on p. 40 of Vol. XII. of the *Corpus Inscriptionum Latinarum*, where the inscription is given in full.

The number of miles, which is always found at the end of the inscription, when specified at all, is here

### XXXIII,

corresponding as near as possible with the actual distance by road from Frejus.

If only the practice of engraving the total distance from the Caput Viae on every milestone had been universal, we should have had an invaluable means of correcting the inaccuracies and discrepancies in the distances given by the Itinerary and Table respectively.

While the Itinerary and the Table give the distances from Forum Julii to Forum Voconii as XII and XVII,

---

[1] In order to prove beyond a doubt that the now banked up central portion of the gateway was formerly open, I had the ground excavated till wheel-ruts, worn in the pebble pavement leading right up to the centre of the structure, were laid bare.

and from Forum Voconii to Matavone as XII and XXII respectively, making a total of XXIV by the Itinerary and XXXIX by the Table, the actual distance is XXXIII as marked on the milestone.

The actual measurement on the milestone also corroborates the statement in the letter of Plancus to Cicero[1] that Forum Voconii was 24 miles from Forum Julii, for Camp-Dumy where the milestone was found is about nine miles from Forum Voconii (le Luc).

The milestone found there is by no means the only evidence of the passage of the Via Aurelia at Camp-Dumy. For I followed the unmistakeable track of the road itself for more than a mile westward from the end of the picturesque mediaeval bridge, replacing the Roman structure, which carried the Via Aurelia over the stream of the Issole, which vies with the Argens in its silvery limpidity.

In the town of Brignolles some 10 miles further west a square-shaped milestone, 6 ft. high, similar to that in the museum at Frejus, is now erected in a market garden formerly within the precincts of a Capuchin monastery. It bears witness to the activity of the Emperor Nero in repairing this portion of the road.

A precisely similar milestone, with a similar inscription—both unfortunately wanting in the item of the total of miles from the Caput Viae—is to be seen on the lofty terrace of the Château of Tourves, splendid even in its ruins, which look down on the town of Tourves, the Roman station of Ad Turrem[2].

Between the Station Ad Turrem and the next, Tegulata (see Section of Peutinger's Table), I walked over the Via Aurelia itself for at least four miles, picking

---

[1] See p. 159.

[2] To my great surprise, and no small satisfaction, I found in the ancient hostelry of St Jean at Tourves (a station on the railway between Carnoulles and Gardanne) a nicely furnished sitting room and clean bedrooms, which combined with the attractions of the ruined Château and its grounds render it the most desirable stopping place between Frejus and Aix-en-Provence.

up the thread of it where it crosses the high road, about a mile to the south of the town of St Maximin.

A facsimile of a milestone erected by the Emperor Claudius (father of Nero by adoption), the original of which is to be seen in the cloister of the Monastery, attached to the magnificent church of St Maximin, has been placed *in situ* on the road, whence the monks removed the original.

The Via Aurelia, in its passage to the south of the town, avoids the plain in which St Maximin lies, by insinuating itself amongst the mountains, the most striking of which is called 'Mont Aurèle'—presumably after the road. The milestone stands at about a mile from the point where the stony track representing the Via Aurelia rejoins the high road from St Maximin to Aix.

On emerging from the mountains, where it crosses the watershed dividing the basin of the Argens from that of the Arc, the Via Aurelia proceeds onwards to Aquae Sextiae across the battle-field of Marius, running between the elongated ridge of the Mont Sainte Victoire and the River Arc for several miles.

From Aquae Sextiae to Arelate[1] (Arles) as is clearly shown in the Table of Peutinger, the Via Aurelia forms a loop, one branch leading by Massilia (Marseilles) and the Fossae Marianae, while the other and more direct passes by Pisavis (near Salon) and across the plain of La Crau. The former is adopted by the Itinerary of Antonine to the exclusion of the latter, whereas both are indicated by the Table of Peutinger, which makes the distance from Aquae Sextiae to Arles 114 miles *via* Marseilles and only 58 *via* Pisavis (Salon).

It is certain that the original Via Domitia followed the latter route, as being the shortest cut from Forum Julii to the Rhone at Arles. To have taken their road as the Itinerary does through Massilia and Greek territory would have been contrary to Roman policy at the date

---

[1] The ancient name for Arles, Arelat*e* (or Arelatum), becomes Arelat*o* in the ablative case, as in the Table of Peutinger.

of its original construction, when Marseilles was an independent Republic and faithful ally of Rome.

As my final contribution towards the elucidation of this intricate question I submit, in tabular form for the sake of clearness, the best conclusions I can arrive at as to the course and nomenclature of the coast-road, styled by the Itinerary of Antonine

## Via Aurelia.

A Roma per Tusciam et Alpes Maritimas Arelatum usque M.P. DCCXCVII.

|  | Original Name | Author | Starting Point | Finishing Point | Date B.C. |
|---|---|---|---|---|---|
| Section 1 | Aurelia | C. Aurelius Cotta | Rome | Vada Volaterrana | 241 |
| ,, 2 | Aemilia Scauri | M. Aemilius Scaurus | Vada Volaterrana | Vada Sabata | 109 |
| ,, 3 | Julia Augusta | Augustus | Vada Sabata | Var | 12 |
| ,, 4 | Massiliensis | Unknown | Var | Forum Julii | 154 |
| ,, 5 | Domitia | Cn. Domitius Ahenobarbus | Forum Julii | Arelate | 121 |

Whether we are justified in calling it Via Aurelia or not, is perhaps of less importance than the fact which is universally admitted, that there was at one time a continuous coast-road from Rome to Arles.

# INDEX.

Actium, battle off, 162
Adige, valley of the, 107
Aduatuci, descended from Cimbri and settled among the Belgae, 103
Aedui, the, 52, 92
Aegytna, oppidum of Oxybii, 80; destruction of, 83
Aelius, P., one of the triumvirate appointed for partitioning land among colonists of Luna, 65
Aemilianus, Fabius Max., commemoration of the victories of, 96
Aemilius Paulus, L., expedition of, 70; Plutarch's life of, 70, 71; death of two of his sons, 71; sortie by, 74–76
Afranius, one of Pompey's legati in Spain, 137
Afridis, the, 65
Agay, 81
Agricola, birthplace of, 88; his mother Julia murdered at Vintimiglia, 88 *note*
Ahenobarbus, Domitius, Proconsul, 92; victory of, 93; capture of Bituitus by, 95; the founder of the Via Domitia, 98, 100; fleet of, 142; governor of the Provincia Narbonensis, 137, 138; summoned to join the fleet of Nasidius, 144; the first road-maker, 166
Aix-en-Provence, battle of, 85, 99
Aix-Pourrières, battle of, 110
Alaudae, legion of the, 136
Albenga, selection of, by Mago, for the base of his operations, 38; council of chiefs at, 39; conquest of the Ingauni at, 69–76
Albici, in the pay of the Massiliots, 141; sorties by the, 143
"Albula" the former name of the Tiber, 48
Alesia, operations around, 136

Allia, defeat of the Romans at the battle of the, 18
Allobroges, factories of the, 33; war with, 92; insurrection of the, 128; complaints of the, against Fonteius, 128; embassy to Rome, 128, 129; Caesar's desire to secure the friendship of the, 132; allies of the Romans, *ib.*; 'Senate' of the, 133; revolt of the, after the death of Caesar, 134
Allobrogicus, Q. Fabius, conquest of Provincia by, 98
Alpine nations, Hasdrubal unmolested by, 36
Alps, Hannibal's passage of the, 27–35; western passes of the, used by the Romans, 32
Ambrones, slaughter of, 85; annihilation of the armies of Caepio and Manlius by the, 104; identity of battle cry used by Ambrones and Ligurians, 113; defeat of the, 113; their reception at the hands of their women, 113, 114
Ambrones and Teutones, preparations of, to cross the Rhone, 109
Andora, bridge at, 174
Antipolis, Greek colony from Massilia, 15; founding of, 79; siege of, 79–83
Antonine Itinerary, 78, 154, 163, 164, 171, 173, 174, 176, 182, 184
Antonius, L., cavalry of, 153, 156
Antonius, Marcus, consul, 150; reception of Octavianus by, 150; defeats of, 151; before Mutina, 151; off Actium, 162; lays siege to Mutina, 151; meeting of, with Lepidus on the river Argens, 156–162; flight into Gallia Narbonensis, 157, 158; arrival at Forum Julii, 158; appointed triumvir, 161; Gaul assigned as province to, 162

# INDEX.   187

Aosta, 31; country of the Salassi, 31
Apennines, the, 77
Apron, the, 80, 82
Apuani, the, 61, 62; defeat of, by Sempronius, 64; transported to the Taurasian plains, 64, 65; deportation of the. 69
Aquae Sextiae, 89, 91, 96, 99; battle of, 109-118 (see also Aix-en-Provence)
Aquae Statiellae, 154
Aquileia, Roman colony at, 73; Decimus Brutus put to death at, 161
Arausio, 90
Arbois de Jubainville, M. d', on the number of Celts in Gallia, 3-5; on the Ligurians, 46, 47, 48; on the Ligurian civilization, 50
Arc, slaughter of Ambrones and Teutones in the valley of, 85; bed of the, 112; Marius's battle in the valley of the, 118
Arecomici, the founders of the Celtic Emporium at Narbonne, 12; a branch of the Volcae, *ib.*
Argens, the, 87; meeting of Antony and Lepidus on, 156-162
Ariminum, 63
Ariovistus, encounter of Julius Caesar with, 110; negotiations with, 121
Arles, native settlement at, 33; in possession of the Salluvii, 87; why not selected as the Roman Capital, 96; depopulation of, 97; a centre of Roman roads, 139; arrival of Caesar's ships from, 142; colony at, 149
Arras, *see* Nemetocenna
Arverni, 12; over-lordship of the, 13; army of the, 92; disaster to the, on the Rhone, 94
Aspres-Veynes, 91
Athenopolis, colony at, 15
Atilius, praetor, 26
Augustus, Liguria or Regio IX. of, 48; altar of, 162; monument in honour of, at Turbia, *ib.*; organization of the Gallic provinces by, *ib.*
Avienus, Festus, *Ora Maritima*, 9, 10; Lacus Ligusticus mentioned by, 49; situation of Marseilles described by, 140
Avignon, native settlement at, 33

Baal, altar of, at Marseilles, 14
Baebius, M., consul, 64; proconsul, 73

Bassus, Ventidius, legate of Antony, 156, 158
Belloguet, Baron Roger de, 'Ethnogénie' Gauloise, 2, 3
Bellovesus, Celts under, 11
Bertrand, A., 11, 47
Bergier, N., on the Roman roads, 166, 167
Bernard, Little St, 31
Besançon, seizure of, by Julius Caesar, 110
Bituitus, King of the Arverni, 93-95
Bituriges, 12
Boii, 12; final subjugation of the, 18; encounter the Romans, 19; resistance of the, 44; expulsion of, from Gallia Cisalpina, 57
Bononia, colony of, 44; Roman colonists around, 51
Bordeaux an imperial residence, 8
Bormida, river, 154
Bourguignat, M., *Les Inscriptions de Vence*, 180
Brancus, supplies to Hannibal by, 29, 33
Briançon, railway, 91
Brignolles, 183
Brittany, population of, mainly Iberian, 8
Brutus, Decimus, takes command of the fleet off Marseilles, 139, 142; triumph of, 143; takes refuge at Modena, 151; letter to Cicero, 152; arrival at Acqui, 157; army of, at Eporedia, 160; desperate condition of, 161; attempts to join Marcus Brutus *ib.*; put to death, *ib.*

Cabasse, village of, 182
Cadibona, 154
Caecilius, C., puts down the revolt of the Salluvii, 121
Caepio, annihilation of the army of, by the Ambrones, 104; possession of gold by, stored at Tolosa, 105
Caesar, Caius Julius, last public act of, affecting the Roman Province, 149; events of the year following the assassination of, 149-155; presence of, on the Riviera, 175
Calvinus, Sextius, 85, 88, 97
Camp-Dumy, 182, 183
Caninius, operations of, 136
Cannae, battle of, 34
Cannes, Roman commissioners put ashore at, 81
Cap Roux, 79, 88, 181
Carbo, Cnaeus, consul, 103

## INDEX.

Carthage, Carthaginian army, composition of, 34; treaty of peace with, 43; final destruction of, 84
Carthaginians, re-establishment of supremacy at sea by the, 15
Castel d' Appio, 72
Catiline conspiracy, 129, 130
Catugnatus, Manlius Lentinus outgeneralled by, 130
Catulus, monument to, at Glanum, 107; consul, 123
Cavaillion, 112
Cavares, confederation of the, 32; plain of the, 90
Celesia, E., on the Ligurians, 46
Celtic, Celtae and Belgae speak the Celtic language, 6
Celts, possession of N.W. Mediterranean coast line by, 9; form a settlement on the Atlantic seaboard of the Iberian peninsula, 10, 11; Ligurians falsely said to be akin to the, 46
Celts and Ligurians, contests between, 10
Cenis, Mont, railway, 30
Cenomani, invasion of eastern Transpadana by the, 48
Cethegus, death of, 129
Cicero, death of, 161, 162
Cimbri, use of caravans by, 9; invasion of the Rhone valley by the, 97; embassy to Augustus from the, 102; destruction of the, at Vercellae, 118
Cimbri and Teutones, German origin of, 102
Cimbro-Teuton invasion, Marius and the, 101-108
Cimiez, 80; Val Laghet, short road to, 176
Cinna, Roman internecine struggles under the leadership of, 120
Claudius, Appius, consul, 71; victories of, 72
Claudius, Emperor, milestone erected by, 184
'Claustra Galliae,' 88
'Claustra maris,' 88
Cleopatra, 162
Clusium, 18
Col de l'Argentière, 31, 32
Col de Tenda, 77
Colonia Julia Viennensis, 134
Constantine, oppidum of, 56; ruins of, *ib.*
Copillus, chief of the Volcae Tectosages, capture of, by Sylla, 104
Cornelius, M., takes up the command of Spurius Lucretius, 140

Cornelius, P., consul, 64
Cotta, Aurelius, 165
Crassus, Licinius, orator, 101
Cremona, military colony at, 19, 20; Hamilcar plans seizure of, 43; siege and relief of, 43; battle of, 43
Critognatus, harangue of, 107, 108

Dawkins, Boyd, *Early Man in Britain*, 8
Dea, 91
Deciates, the, 79, 80; subjection of, 83
Delphi, treasure of, 7; spoil of Veii in the Massiliot treasury at, 16; sack of, 102
Dertona, 152, 153
Dervieu, Captain, on the campaign of Marius, 115
Dolabella, P. Cornelius, consul, 150
'Dolmen,' near Draguignan, 53
Donzère, 25
Drac, 31
Drappes, 136
Drôme, junction of, with the Rhone, 25; valley of the, 91
Durance valley, 3, 29, 30, 36, 90-96

Egus, 133
Eighty Years' War, 57, 58
Elba, the Ligurian 'Ilva,' 47
Emporiae, 98
Encourdoules, 81
Entremont, discoveries of bas-reliefs at, 53, 54; description of, 53, 54, 55; hot springs, 112
Epanterii Montani, the, 38, 39; join the Ingauni, 72; treachery of the allies, 73
Eporedia, army of Decimus Brutus at, 160
Eratosthenes, fragment of, 49
Esterel, the, 79, 157, 158
Etang de Berre, 21, 56, 87
Etruria, Cisalpine Gauls in, 18
Etruscans, defeat of, off Cumae, 15; driven from the Po valley, 18
Etrusco-Carthaginian naval alliance, 15

Fabius Maximus, Q., consul, 92
Fasti Capitolini, 87, 88, 90, 121
Flaccus, Fulvius, consul, 84, 85, 86, 87, 88, 90; conquest of Provincia begun by, 98
Flaccus, Valerius, triumph of, over Gauls and Celtiberians, 121

# INDEX.

Flaminius, Caius, consul, 62; commissioner, 80; wounded, 81
Fonteius, M., charge of appropriating moneys against, 98; Cicero's oration on behalf of, 126, 127, 128
Forum Aurelii, 165
Forum Julii, 87, 88, 96, 98, 99, 149, 157, 158, 179-182
Forum Voconii, 159, 160, 182, 183
Fos, vestiges of Roman camp at, 106
France, ancient, derived its name from the Galli, 2; majority of inhabitants of, not of Gallic origin, *ib.*; race-feud between French and Germans not to be attributed to Celtic element, *ib.*; modern, German Franks give the name to, *ib.*; S.W. quarter of, mainly Iberian, 13
Frejus, bay of, 87; colony at, 149; museum at, 181
Freshfield, D., Alpine Pass of Hannibal, 31, 32
Friniates, the, 61, 62
Fulvia, wife of Antony, 162

Gaesatae, Transalpine, 39
Galba, Servius Sulpicius, secures triumph for Pomptinus, 130
Gallia, early distribution of races in Gaul, 1; traces of pre-historic man in Gaul, 1; M. d'Arbois de Jubainville, on the number of Celts in Gallia, 3-5; derivation of the name, 2; ancient, distribution of the population in, 6; modern, ground-work of the population Iberian, 5; divisions of, 5, 6; distinctions of language existing in, 5
Gallia Cisalpina, derives her main contingent of Gauls from the valley of the Danube, 12; contest of the Romans with, 17; critical state of affairs in, 18; subjugation of, 19; invasion of, by Hasdrubal and Mago, 36-44; real beginning of Roman administration in, 44; beginning of military road construction in, 62, 63
Gallia Comata, 132, 134, 162
Gallia Narbonensis, 121
Gallia Transalpina, Iberian, Ligurian and Celtic races found in, 9; never the parent hive of Celts, 11; theory of reflux of Gauls from, not altogether to be rejected, 12; first Roman blood shed in, 23

Gallic irruptions, special fund provided to meet, 19
Gallinara, island of, seizure by Mago, 38
Gallus, meaning of, 86
Gap, 91
Gauls, types of, 6, 7; Romans derive their knowledge of, from Belgica, 7; occupy north-eastern and central plateaus of France, 10; sacking and burning of Rome by the, 18
Gauls and Ligurians, the main constituents of Hannibal's army, 34; insurrection of, 43
Genèvre, Pass of Mt, 31, 125
Genoa, descent on, by Mago, 38; few traces of Romans at, 52; relations with Rome and Marseilles, 52; sacking and burning of, *ib.*; no coins of earlier date than Roman conquest found there, 53
Gentes Alpinae, 78
Genuatae, the, 52, 70
Gergovia, plateau of, 93; repulse of the Romans from, 132
German slaves in Italy, 118
Germania Superior and Inferior, 8
Glanum, Roman camp at, 107, 109
Goorkhas, the, 76
Gracchus, Caius, 84
Greece, invasion of, by Gauls, 7
Greek element, introduction of, into the population of Gallia Transalpina, 13
Gretia, name given to the region between Marseilles and the Durance, 13; mentioned in the table of Peutinger, 137
Guadiana, river, 49

Hamilcar, insurrection of Gauls and Ligurians at the instigation of, 43; death of, 43
Hannibal in the Rhone valley, 17-26; Passage of Alps, 27-35, 82; infantry and cavalry of the army of, 33; delay of, in the country of the Allobroges, and its consequences, 33; loss of an eye by, 38; final defeat of, at Zama, 42; sets sail to Carthage, 42
Hanno, 23
Hasdrubal, favourable reception of, 36; invasion of Cisalpine Gaul by Hasdrubal and Mago, 36-44; defeat and death of, 37
Hecataeus, 49
Hercules, Pillars of, 11, 15

# INDEX.

Hesperides, modern gardens of the, 175
Himera, battle of, 15, 49
Himilco, Carthaginian navigator, 9
Hirschfeld, on the Via Aurelia, 166
Hirtius, Aulus, consul, 151
Hirtuleius, quaestor of Sertorius, 124
Histria, war in, 73
Hyères, 89

Iberian family, the Ligurians a branch of the, 45
Iberians, possession of N.W. Mediterranean coast line by, 9; non-resistance by, within the limits of Gaul, 10
Illiberis, 32
Ilvates, the, 48
Ingauni, the, alliance of Mago with, 38; conquest of the, at Albium Ingaunorum, 69–76; treachery of, 73
Insubres, 12, 19
Intemelii, co-operation of the, with the Ingauni, 72; subjection of the, 77
Ireland, change of language in, 8
Isère, junction of the, with the Rhone, 25; Hannibal's passage of the, 27, 28, 29
Italy, attempted barbarian invasion of, 86

Jugurthine war, 104
Julia, wife of Marius, 111
Junonia, colony of, 84

La Croix de Garde, 180
Laghet, valley of, 176; monastery of, 177
Laterensis, senator, suicide of, 160
La Turbie, pass, 58; inscription on the monument of, 80
Laval, plain of, 180
Lazarus, first legendary Bp of Marseilles, 121
Lentheric, M., description of Tauroenta by, 144; on the Via Aurelia, 165, 166; on the Via Julia Augusta, 171; on the Via Aurelia, 176
Lentinus, Manlius, out-generalled by Catugnatus, 130
Lentulus, death of, 129
Lepidus, M. Aemilius, *the elder*, elected consul, 122, 123; proconsul of Provincia, 123; defeat and death of, 123; the Triumvir, 161; letter to Cicero, 159; meeting of Antony and, on the river Argens, 156–162
Lerici and Turbia, coast road between, 173
Les Baux, bas-relief of the "Tre Marie" at, 121
Les Maures, mountains of, 87
Lex Pedia, 161
Libica, the name of the two most westerly mouths of the Rhone, 48
Libui, the, 48
Ligures capillati, 51, 52
Ligures tonsi, 51, 52
Liguria, early distribution of races in, 1; traces of pre-historic man in, 1; withdrawal of Hannibal to, 35; invasion of, by Hasdrubal and Mago, 36–44; Carthaginian attempt to create diversion in, 37; Eastern campaigns in, 57–68; Transalpine, conquest of, 77–88
Ligurian, the, 80 years' war, 78
Ligurian *oppida* in Provence, 53
Ligurians, the, 45–56; possession of N.W. Mediterranean coast line by, 9; of Western Riviera, internecine warfare of, 38; the oldest family in Western Europe, 45; two kinds of, 51; nothing known of the religious observances of, 53; defeat by Aemilius Paulus, 76; identity of battle cry used by Ambrones and Ligurians, 113
"Ligusticus, Lacus," 49
"Ligustine" city, 49
Ligyes, the, 48, 49
Livia, wife of Tib. Claudius Nero, and afterwards of Augustus, mother of Emperor Tiberius, 149
Livius, M., prolongation of the "Imperium" of, 40
Livy's date as to appearance of Celts in Italy rejected, 11; on Hannibal's Passage, 29–31; names preserved by, in connection with Hannibal's march from the Pyrenees to the Alps, 32
Longinus, Cassius, destruction of the army of, 103
Lucan, *Pharsalia*, Book III., specimen from Rowe's version of the sea-fight, 145, 146
Lucretius, Spurius, prolongation of "Imperium" of, 40
Lucterius, 136

# INDEX.

Lucus, 91

Lumone, Roman Station of, 175

Luna, an Etruscan city, 65; colony of, 65, 66, 67

Lyons, Roman colony at, 134; the Roman capital of Gallia Comata, 162

Magalus, a chief of the Boii, 24

Mago, invasion of Cisalpine Gaul by Hasdrubal and, 36–44; attempt to retrieve Hannibal's fortunes by, 37; swims the Po, 37; battle at the Trebia decided by, 37; wounded, 41; death of, 42; Genoa singled out for attack by, 52; abandonment of the Ingauni by, 71

Mallius, L., proconsul of Provincia, 123; summoned to Spain, *ib.*; defeat there, 123, 124

Mancinus, C. Hostilius, consul, 158

Manlius, praetor, 26; annihilation of the army of, by the Ambrones, 104

Mantua defended by its surrounding marshes, 18

Marcellus, ambuscade of, 115, 117

Marcius, L., consul, 63; disaster to the army of, 64

Marengo, battlefield of, 155

Maria, association of the name of, with Marius, 121

Marian faction, 122, 123

Marius, annihilation of the Ambrones and Teutones by, 52; Italian Ligurians in the army of, 76; confidence of the people in, 104; monument to, at Glanum, 107; successes of, over the Ambrones and Teutones, 114–117; fall of, 117, 118; triumphal monument of, 118; secret letters of, to the chiefs, 120; Roman internecine struggles under the leadership of, *ib.*; still a popular name in Provence, *ib.*

Marius and the Cimbro-Teuton invasion, 101–108

Martha, a Syrian prophetess, 111, 121

Martha, association of the name of, with Marius, 121

Marseilles, discovery of stone tablet at, 13; foundation of, 13, 14, 15; rapid rise of commerce of, 15; places of honour reserved for the Massiliots at public games in Rome, 16; commercial prosperity of, due to the Romans, 16;
mutual services rendered between Marseilles and Rome, *ib.*; situation of, 21; foundation of, 49; founding of 'Antipolis' by the Massiliots, 79; governing body of, 138, 139; defeat of the fleet of, 146; siege and blockades of, 137–148; violation by the Massiliots of the armistice granted by the Romans, 147; surrender of the city, 148

Massilia, *see* Marseilles

Matienus, C., naval force under, 73; victory of, 76

Maximus, Quintus Fabius, consul, 71, 92; victory of, 93; triumph of, 95; honours, *ib.*

'Menhir' near Brignolles, 53

Mercury, statue of the Arverne, 93

Metaurus, battle of the river, 37

Milan, falls into the hands of the Romans, 19

Milestones, 177, 178, 179, 180, 181, 182, 183, 184

Milvian bridge, battle at, 123; arrest of conspirators at, 129

Mistral, the, 147

Modena, siege of, by Marc Antony, 151

Mommsen, Th., on Hannibal's Passage, 30; on the Via Aurelia, 165; composition of the route from Rome to the Var, 172

Monaco, Greek colony from Massilia, 15

Moneglia (Ad Monilia), 70

Montelimar, 25

Müllenhof, K., on the Ligurians, 45–47

Mutina, colony of, 44

Mutina, *see also* Modena

Napoleon I., on the secret of Roman successes, 74

Napoule (Ad Horrea), 181

Narbo Martius, colony of, 127

Narbonensis, Provincia, 59

Narbonne, Celtic Emporium at, 12; colonization of, 84; Roman endeavour to secure land thoroughfare to, 99; colony at, 101, 149

Nasidius, L., sent to the relief of the Massiliots, 143, 144; cowardice of the navy of, 145, 146

Nemetocenna (Arras), Caesar's last winter in Gaul spent at, 136

Nero, Claudius, consul, 37

Nero, Tiberius Claudius, sent by Caesar to plant colonies in Gaul, 149

Nicaea, colony at, 15, 79; siege of, *ib.*
Nîmes, native settlement at, 33
Numantia, siege and capture of, 50, 84, 98
Numatianus, Rutilius, on his return journey from Rome to Gaul, 173
Numidians attack Scipio's cavalry, 23

Octavianus, claims of, 150, 151; marches into Gallia Cisalpina, 151; elected consul, 160; gets the 'Lex Pedia' passed, 161; appointed Triumvir, 161
Octavius, Cnaeus, capture of Mago's merchantmen by, 39
Olbia, colony at, 15
Olympus, Mt, 116
Opimius, Quintus, consul, 80, 81; camp of, 82; campaign of, 88; conquest of territory by, 99
Orange, 24, 25
Orba, river, 154, 155
Orgon, 111, 112
Orosius, supposed acquaintance with the lost books of Livy by, 60
Oxybii, the, 79, 80, 81, 83, 87, 88

Pain de Munition, 55, 56, 114, 115
Pansa, Vibius, consul, 151
Papiria, wife of Aemilius Paulus, 70; divorce, 71
Parma, colony of, 44
Pedius, Quintus, consul, 160
Perperna, legate of M. Lepidus, senior, 123
Petreius, 137
Peutinger, Table of, 13, 137, 154, 163, 164, 174, 176, 184
Philistus, on the Ligurians, 48
Phocaeans, 21
Picenates, 156
Pisa, Roman colonists around, 51; Roman milestone in the Campo Santo at, bearing the name of Via Aemilia, 167
Pisae, 60, 61
Piso, Calpurnius, insurrection of the Allobroges quelled by, 128
Piso, Lucius, 103
Pitot, J. J. A., "Recherches sur les Antiquités Dauphinoises," 132, 133
Placentia, military colony planted at, 19, 20; failure of Hannibal to get possession of, 35; siege of the fortress of, by Hasdrubal, 37; Hamilcar plans seizure of, 43; destruction of, by Hamilcar, 43;
recovery of its position as Roman centre in Cisalpine Gaul, 44
Plancus, L. Munatius, governor of Gallia Ulterior, 134; letter to Cicero, 158, 159, 183; returns to Grenoble, 160; abandons Cicero, *ib.*
Po, the, swum by Mago, 37
Po valley, Etruscans driven from, 18; Hasdrubal's unexpected arrival, 36
Polcevere, river of Genoa, 53
Polybius, incompetence of, as a geographer, 27, 28; Four Passes of, 32
Pompey, opening of the pass of Mt Genèvre by, 31; crossing of the Cottian Alps by, 91; reputation of, 124; summoned to the rescue of Italy, *ib.*; letter to the Roman Senate, 124, 125, 126; his passage across the Alps, 124, 125
Pomptinus, C., insurrection of the Allobroges quelled by, 128, 130; triumph voted for, 130, 131; final subjugation of the Allobroges by, 133
Pons Argenteus, 160
Pont Flavien, at St Chamas, 56
Ponte Lungo, 174
Porcius, L., praetor, 36
Porta Aurelia, 165
Porta Decumana, 75
Porta Flaminia, 63
Porta Gallica, 88, 182
Porta Praetoria, 75
Porta Principalis, 75
Porta Romana, 181, 182
Portus Herculis Monoeci (Monaco), 78
Portus Lunae, 67
Poseidonius, on the habits of the Ligurian natives, 50
Pourrières, defeat of the Teutones near, 114–117; relics from the battle field, 118
Procillus, Caius Valerius, Roman franchise conferred on, 121
Provence, never occupied or conquered by Gauls, 13; Ligurian oppida in, 53
Provincia, conquest of, 97, 98, 99; misgovernment of, 120; colonization of, 121, 122; its situation, 122; Gallic element in, 127; in relation to Caesar's Gallic and Civil Wars, 132–139
Provincia Narbonensis, administration of, 162

# INDEX.

"Provincia Romana," 5
Punic War, First, 16, 17; Second, 17, 36, 37; Third, 84
Punic Wars, 11
Puy de Dôme, 93

Quiliano, 153, 154
Quintana, 153

Raucillus, friend of Caesar, 133
Réclus, E., on the Ligurians, 45
Red Rocks, cave dwellings of the, 175
Reinach, S., 11
Renan, E., on the existence of a previous Phoenician settlement at Marseilles, 14
Reno, river, 161
Rhone, the, a dividing line between the Iberians and Ligurians, 10; difficult navigation of, 22; cutting of a new mouth to the, 106
Rhone valley, Hannibal in the, 17–26; physical features of, 33; invasion of, by the Cimbri and Teutones, 97
Rigi-Culm, 125
Riviera, Italian, Ligurians of the, 50, 51
'Riviera di Levante,' 69
Roman Province, the, from the victory of Marius to the proconsulship of Julius Caesar, 119–131
Romans, allies of the Massiliots, 16; defeat of, at the battle of the Allia, 18
Romans and Ligurians, first fighting, 57
Rome, burning of, 16, 18, 101, 102; date of the institution of a standing army at, 105
Roquebrune, 88
Roquemaure, 26
Rossi, G., Storia de Vintimiglia, 175 note
Ruscino, township, 32

Sabatii, Roman alliance with the, 70
St Cassien, hillock of, 180
St Chamas, 56
St Charles, hill of, 140
St Maximin, 184
St Pierre d'Albigny, 28, 30
St Roche, chapel of, 175
Sainte Victore, Mt, 112, 115, 116
Salamis, battle of, 14
Sallust, on the Passage of Hannibal, 31

Salluvii, the, 13, 49, 53, 79, 80, 86, 87, 89, 97, 121
Salyes, the, see Salluvii
Savona, Mago withdraws to, 38
Scaurus, Aemilius, 63, 152
Scipio Aemilianus, 50
Scipio Africanus, rescue of Publius Scipio by, 34; final defeat of Hannibal by, 42
Scipio Africanus, *the younger*, siege and capture of Numantia by, 98
Scipio, Cnaeus, sent to Spain with army by Publius Scipio, 26
Scipio Nasica, final subjugation of the Boii by, 18; ends the resistance of the Boii, 44; cruelty of, *ib.*
Scipio, Publius Cornelius, consul, 17, 18; detaches one of the legions intended for Spain to assist the Romans in Cisalpine Gaul, 20; disembarks at the mouth of Marseilles, 21, 23; sails to Genoa, 26
Scrivia, the, 53
Sembola, Monte, 177
Sempronius, disaster of Marcius avenged by, 64; consul, 71
Sempronius, Tiberius, consul, 17, 18; rashness of, 34
Sena Gallica, Roman colony, 19
Senones, extermination of, from Roman territory, 19
Sertorius, rebellion of, in Spain, 97; Radical faction take service under, 122; supplies to, by Perperna, 123; attempt of, to cross the Alps frustrated by Pompey, 124
Servile War, the, 117, 119, 120
Sestri-Levante, 69
Sezze, commune of, 154, 155
Siagne, river, 79
Sicinius, Cn., triumvir, 65
Sigovesus, Celts under, 11
Sikhs, the, compared to the Ingauni, 76
Silanus, M. Junius, defeat of, 110
Silures, 8, 9
Spain, Carthaginian power in, 17; Roman endeavour to secure land thoroughfare to, 99
Spezia, harbour of, 67
Strabo, Celts and Germans are of kindred blood, 2; divisions of Gaul, 6; comparison of Gauls and Germans by, 7; former extension of Iberia, 10; extension of the over-lordship of the Arverni, 12, 13; on the Via Aemilia, 167
Strada Romana, 168, 169, 174, 175
Stura, valley of the, 32

# INDEX

Sylla, capture of Copillus by, 104; Roman internecine struggles under the leadership of, 120; proscriptions of, 122; death of, *ib.*
Syrian prophetess in the army of Marius, 111

Tauroenta, battle at, 144, 145
Tauroentum, Greek colony at, 15
Tectosages, the ancestors of the Galatians, 7 *note*; a branch of the Volcae, 12
Terillus, tyrant of Himera, 11
Teutomalius, King of the Salluvii, 92, 95
Teuton priestesses, 111
Teutones, use of caravans by, 9; annihilation of, 52, 114; slaughter of, 85; invasion of the Rhone valley by the, 97
Teutones and Ambrones, preparations of, to cross the Rhone, 110; encampment of, and fight with the Romans, 112
Thierry, Amédée, *Histoire des Gaulois*, 1, 7
Ticinus, the, cavalry encounter near, 34, 37
Tigurini, Helvetian, 103
Timaeus, on the date of the original settlement of Marseilles, 14
Tortona, *see* Dertona
Toulouse, massacre of the Roman garrison at Tolosa, 105; outbreak of the Volcae Tectosages at, 120
Tourves, 183
Trajectus Rhodani, 30, 97, 98
Trasimene Lake, battle of, 62
Trebia, victory of the Carthaginians at the, 34; battle at the, decided by Mago, 37
Trebonius, Caius, takes over the siege operations of Marseilles by land, 139; volunteers furnished by, 142
Tricastini, the, 32
Triumvirate, Octavianus, M. Antonius, and M. Lepidus appointed a, 161
Tricorii, the, 33
Turbia, monument to Augustus at, 162
Turin (Taurini), descent of Hannibal on, 32

Umbria, Cisalpine Gauls in, 18
Uvezes, river, 91
Uxellodunum, siege and capture of, 136

Var, the, 79
Vada Sabata, 70, 82, 152, 153, 156, 167, 174
Vada Volaterrana, 164, 165, 167
Varro, on the Passage of Hannibal, 31; Five Passes of, 32
Varus, Q., takes up the command of M. Livius, 40
Vediantii, the, 80
Veii, spoil of, 16
Ventidius, Antony's lieutenant, 153; junction of the army of, with Antony, 159
Vercellae, destruction of the Cimbri at, 118
Vercingetorix, struggle of the Arverni under, 96; Caesar's victory over, 119; attack on Vienna by, 135; defeated by Caesar, 135, 136; surrender, 136
Via Aemilia Lepidi, 63, 168, 172
Via Aemilia Scauri, 70, 152–156, 168–170
Via Aurelia, 99, 100, 152, 163–185
Via Domitia, 96, 98, 99, 166, 184
Via Flaminia, 63, 129, 168, 172
Via Heraclea, 98
Via Julia Augusta, 81, 170–177
Via Levata, 154, 155
Via Massiliensis, 179
Via Postumia, 53, 152, 173
Via Principalis, 75
Via Quintana, 75
Via Vintiana, 180
Vienna, native settlement at, 33; the chief settlement of the Allobroges, *ib.*; colony at, 133; importance of, to Caesar, 134; description of, 134, 135
Vintimiglia, 77, 79, 88 *note*, 175
Villefranche, 78
Vindalium, Allobroges defeated at, 92
Vocontii, the, 32, 90, 91, 131
Volcae established on the Mediterranean sea-board, 12; clients of the Arverni, 13; tribes of the, recorded in Livy, 32
Volcae Arecomici, 90, 95
Volcae Tectosages, rebellion of the, 105, 120

Wales, population of, mainly Iberian, 8
Welsh, derivation of the name, 12
Waterloo, 116

Zama, defeat of Hannibal at, 42

ROMAN AQUEDUCT AT FREJUS (FORUM JULII).

THE RHONE, NEAR ROQUEMAURE WHERE HANNIBAL CROSSED

PASS OF SAN BERNARDO IN THE APENNINES BEHIND ALBENGA.

A

B

BAS-RELIEFS FOUND IN RUINS OF LIGURIAN "OPPIDUM," ENTREMONT, ENVIRONS OF AIX-EN-PROVENCE.

ANCIENT WALL AND RAISED FOOTWAY AT ENTREMONT.

GULF OF FREJUS AND VALLEY OF RIVER ARGENS WITH VIEW OF MONT ROQUEBRUNE.

VILLAGE OF 'FOS' (FOSSA MARIANA) AT MOUTH OF RHONE.

MONT SAINTE VICTOIRE AND ENVIRONS OF AIX-EN-PROVENCE

ROMAN ARCH AT SUSA, ERECTED BY KING COTTIUS IN HONOUR OF AUGUSTUS.

TEMPLE OF AUGUSTUS AND LIVIA AT VIENNE-EN-DAUPHINÉ.

ROMAN BRIDGE, ON VIA JULIA AUGUSTA, BETWEEN VADO AND CADIBONA.—THE VILLAGE SEEN THROUGH THE ARCH.

MEDIAEVAL BRIDGE, REPLACING ROMAN PONS ARGENTEUS.

PONTE LUNGO, NEAR ALBENGA

ROMAN MILESTONE IN VALLEY OF LAGHET, NEAR NICE.

ARLES FROM THE RHONE

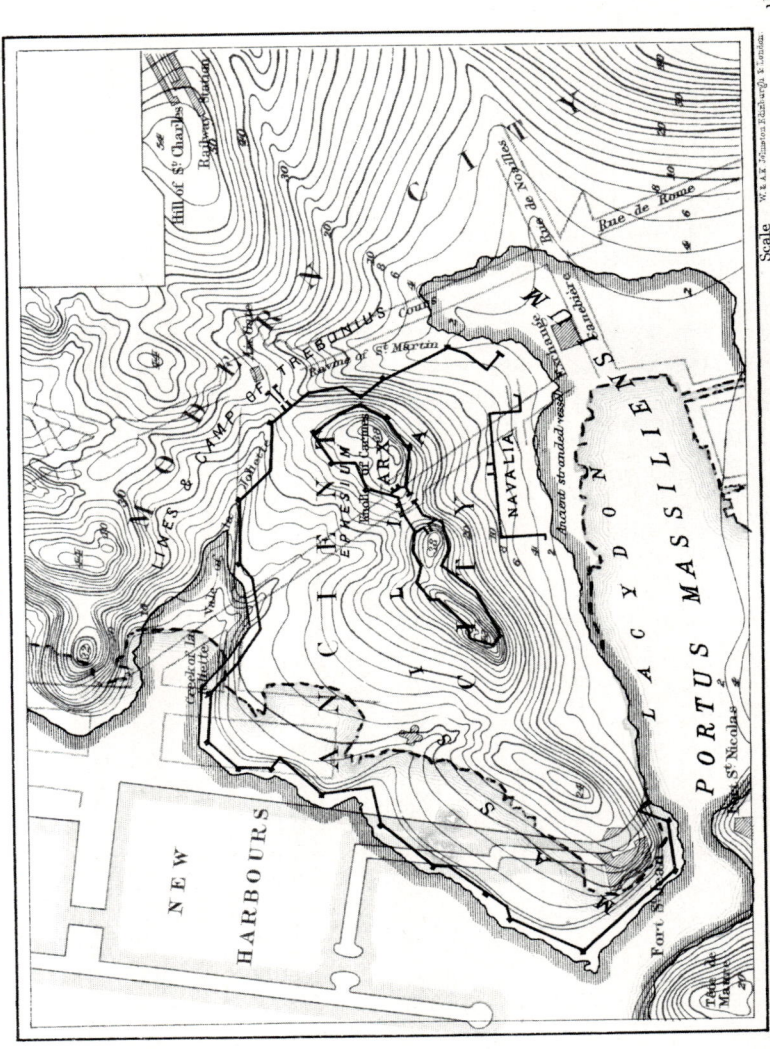

"Massilia enim fere ex tribus oppidi partibus mari alluitur".
— *J. Cæsar: De Bello Civili, Lib. II., c. 1.*

**ANCIENT AND MODERN CITIES AND HARBOURS OF MASSILIA (MARSEILLES).**
*Modern shore line in Blue, ancient in Black.*
▙ *Line of Ancient City Wall.*

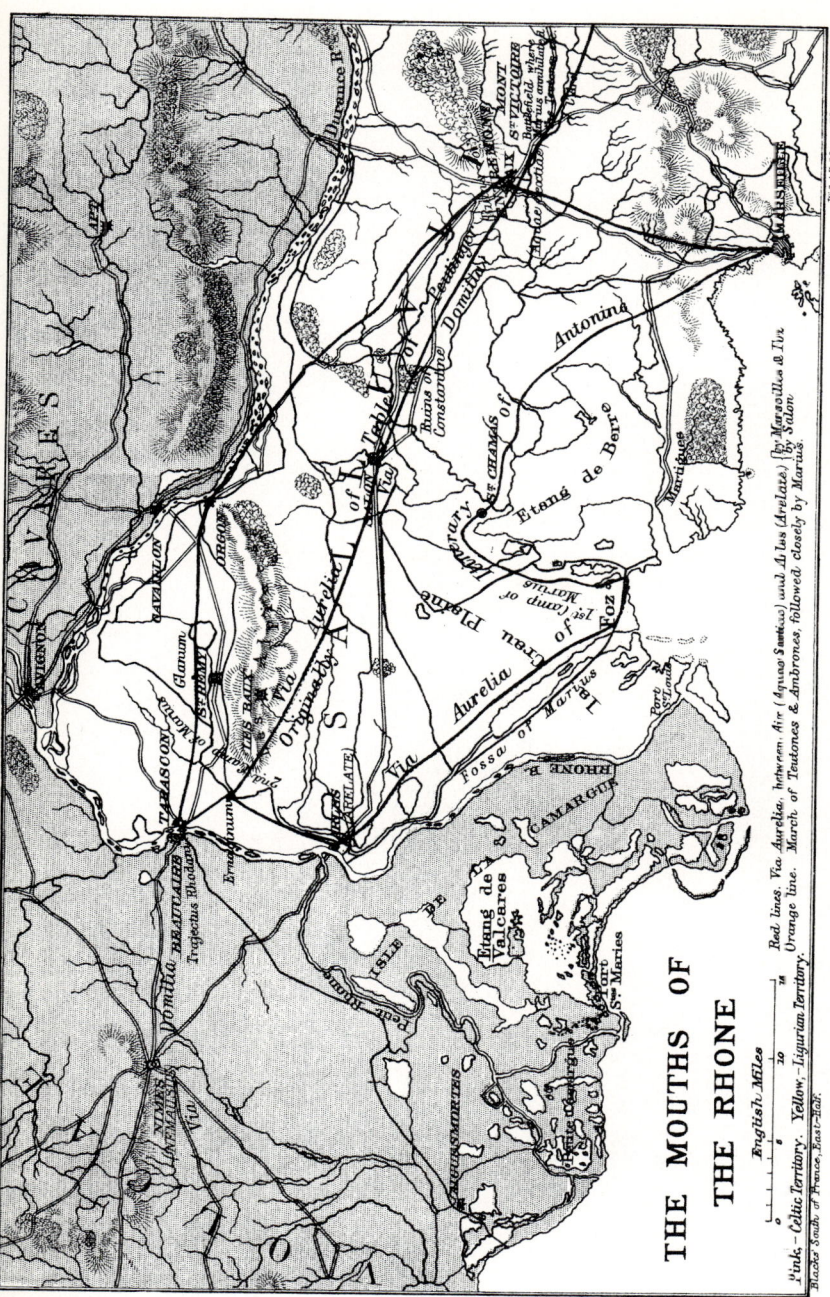

THE MOUTHS OF THE RHONE

DISTRIBUTION OF NATIVE POPULATION AT DATE OF ROMAN CONQUEST OF PROVINCIA
AND FOUNDATION OF AIX B.C. 122 AND OF NARBONNE B.C. 118

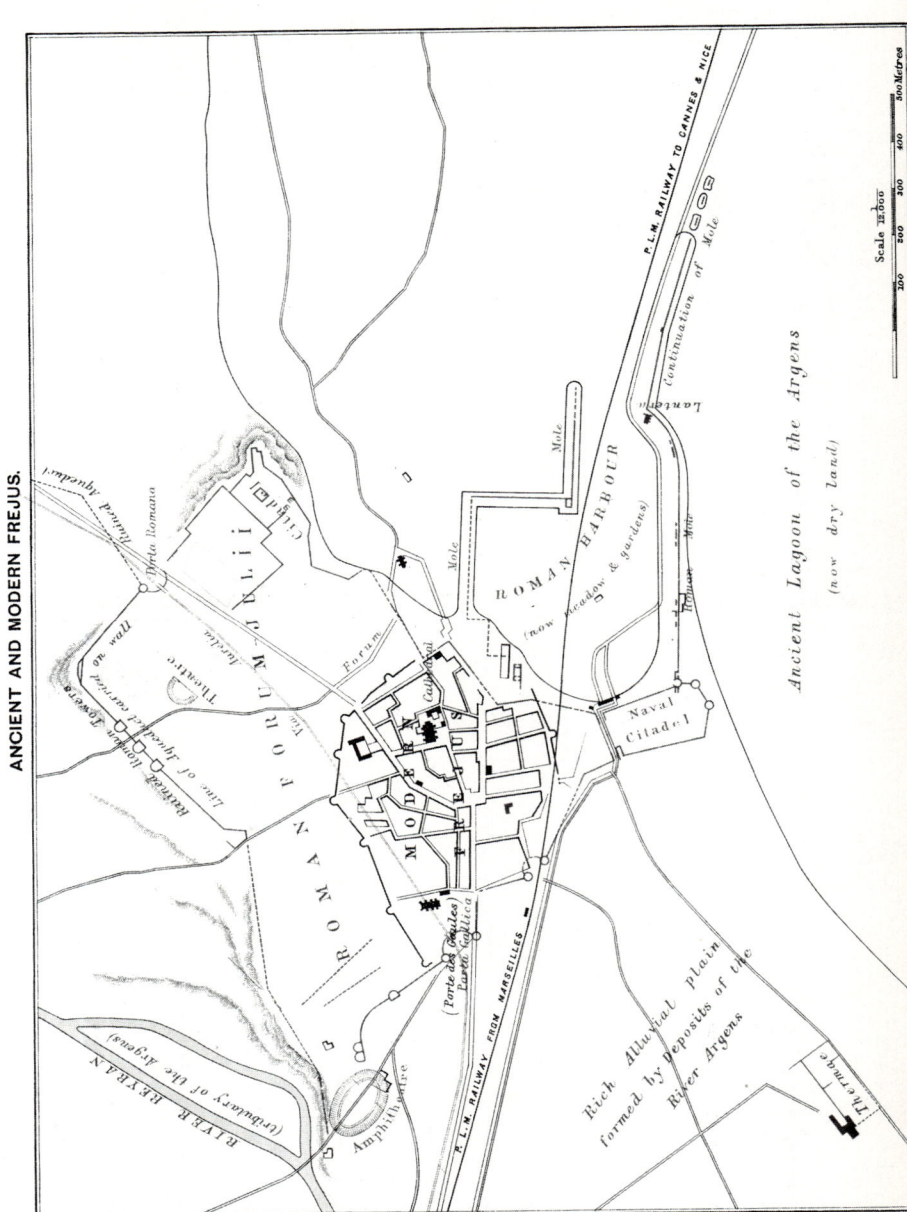

ANCIENT AND MODERN FREJUS.

The Red Colouring shows the boundary of Roman Forum-Julii and its excavated harbour, into which the galleys captured at Actium (B.C. 31)

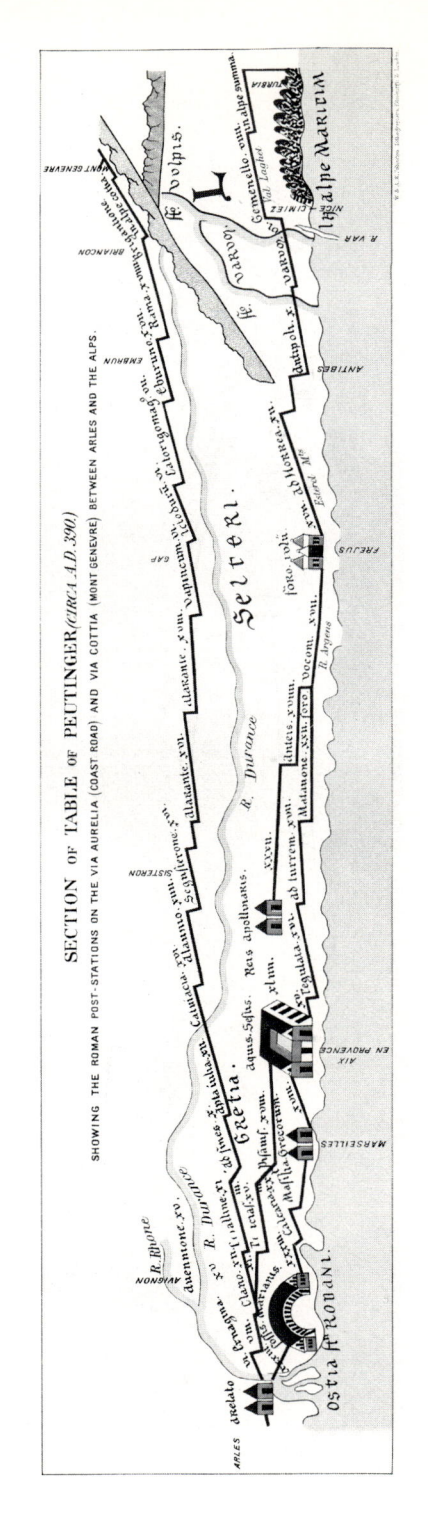

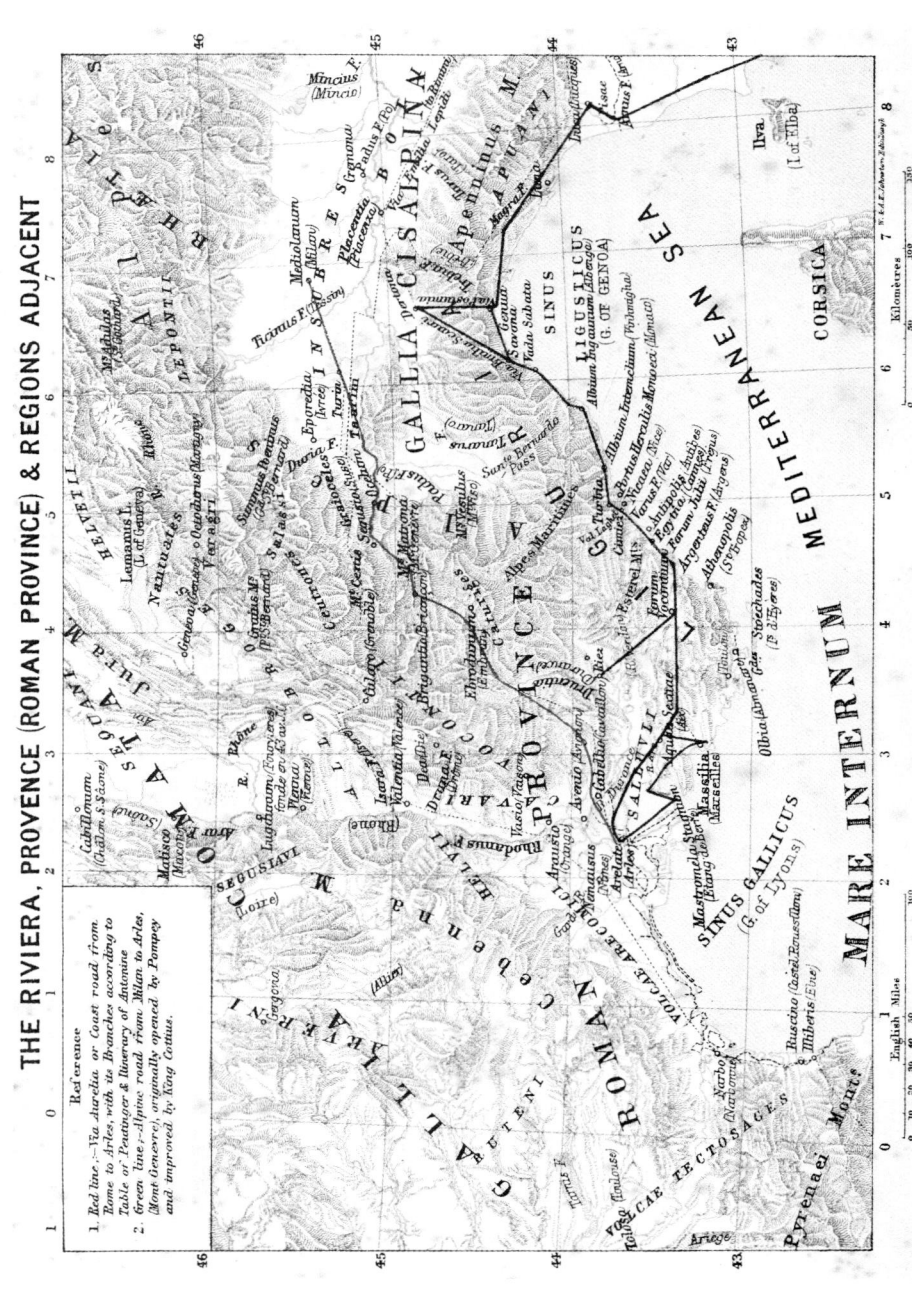